BLAST THE BUSH

LEN BEADELL

BLAST THE BUSH

NEW HOLLAND

Books by Len Beadell:
Too Long in the Bush
Blast the Bush
Bush Bashers
Still in the Bush
Beating About the Bush
Outback Highways (a selection)
End of an Era

Published in Australia by
New Holland Publishers (Australia) Pty Ltd
Sydney • Auckland • London • Cape Town

1/66 Gibbes Street Chatswood NSW 2067 Australia
218 Lake Road Northcote Auckland New Zealand
86 Edgware Road London W2 2EA United Kingdom
80 McKenzie Street Cape Town 8001 South Africa

First published in 1967
First published by Seal Books 1973
Reprinted 1974, 1976
Limp edition 1986
Reprinted 1989
Reprinted by Lansdowne Publishing Pty Ltd 1998, 1999
Reprinted by New Holland Publishers (Australia) Pty Ltd in 2000, 2003, 2004, 2006, 2009

National Library of Australia Cataloguing-in-Publication Data:

Beadell, Len, 1923–
Blast the bush.

ISBN 978-1-86436-736-2

1. Beadell, Len, 1923–. 2. Atomic bomb–South Australia–
Maralinga–testing. I. Title.

355.8251190994238

Wholly designed and typeset in Australia
Printed in Australia by McPherson's Printing Group

10 9 8

LEN BEADELL, who has been called the last of the true Australian explorers, was born on a farm at West Pennant Hills, NSW, in 1923. After showing an interest in surveying at the age of twelve under the guidance of his surveyor scoutmaster, he began his career on a military mapping project in northern NSW in the early stages of World War II. A year later he enlisted in the Army Survey Corps, serving in New Guinea until 1945.

While still in the Army after the war he accompanied the first combined scientific expedition of the CSIRO into the Alligator River country of Arnhem Land in the Northern Territory, fixing the location of discoveries by astronomical observations. Later, after waiving his Army discharge for a further term, he agreed to carry out the initial surveys needed to establish the Woomera rocket range. It was this decision that was to lead to a lifetime of camping, surveying, exploring and roadmaking in the vast empty areas of Central Australia, opening up for the first time more than 2.5 million square kilometres of the Great Sandy, Gibson and Great Victoria Deserts. He chose the site for the first atomic bomb trials at Emu and for the later atomic tests at Maralinga.

As Range Reconnaissance Officer at the Weapons Research Establishment he was awarded the British Empire Medal in 1958 for his work in building the famous Gunbarrel Highway, still the only East-West road link which stretches 1600 kilometres across Central Australia.

In 1987 he became a Fellow of the Institute of Engineering and Mining Surveyors (Aust.) and in the same year astronomers at the Mount Palomar Observatory in California honoured him by naming a newly discovered asteroid planet after him in recognition of the road network he created which made access to the meteorite impact craters they were studying possible. In 1988 he was awarded the medal of the Order of Australia in the Queen's Birthday Honours list.

The author of six best-selling books about his experiences in outback Australia, Len Beadell died in 1995. His three children, Connie-Sue, Gary and Jackie, all have features of outback Australia named after them.

To Our Children
Connie Sue, Gary, and Jacqueline

FOREWORD

With the successful firing of the first British atomic device in the Monte Bello Islands, off the Western Australian coast, in 1952, there arose an urgent need to test two low yield devices as part of the weapon development programme.

On my way back to England I presented to the Australian Government Departments responsible the difficult task of finding a remote area and providing the logistic support for these tests within less than a year. It was apparent that this requirement would involve a considerable airlift, and that a flat clear area had to be found capable of taking medium size freighter aircraft and with a high guarantee that it would not be flooded by rain during the operation.

I can imagine now that, faced with the problem, someone in the Department of Supply must immediately have said "Send for Lennie."

It has often been remarked that, with the uniformity and conformity that modern day civilization imposes, the individualistic characters of past ages no longer emerge. But Lennie, who was at home in the limitless boundaries of the Australian bush, and whose heavy field boots seldom tramped a pavement, developed and retained his own unique character. This I learnt as soon as I arrived in August 1953 to direct our tests at the site he had chosen, known as the Emu Claypan.

A short time after Lennie had chosen the site, an Australian Task Force had moved in under the direction of Brigadier Lucas and, with nothing to spare in time or equipment, had with great resource and sheer physical effort built the scientific and administrative facilities needed for the tests.

Despite the magnitude of the job, the Task Force found time to consider how they could welcome, and make bush life a little easier for, the "Boffins from England." As part of this process they prepared a booklet called "Welcome to the Claypan" illustrated by Lennie, a talented cartoonist. The cover showed a Bristol aircraft that had landed on the Claypan. From behind mulga trees some of the Task Force, each with the attendant cloud of flies that one had to learn to live with, peered out in astonished horror at descending Boffins arrayed in a variety of garb ranging from natty city suiting with bowler hat to riding boots, breeches, and topee, and surrounded by a paraphernalia of cabin trunks, golf clubs, and even a pair of skis. I believe that, at the time, one was actually seen carrying an umbrella. On the walls of the nissen hut used as a dining room, Lennie had drawn two large charcoal murals. One, representing Australiana, was the head of a grinning Aborigine. The other was Lennie's caricature of the average Briton and was of a half-bald, mous-tached, long-nosed character wearing half-moon spectacles. In one detail Lennie's imagination had failed: he had tried to include a butterfly collar but had drawn it upside down. These murals were carefully preserved when the tests were over and now adorn a laboratory at Aldermaston in Berkshire.

These gentle leg pulls were a happy beginning for the scientists who, although having a pallor from the long hours in their laboratories preparing for these experiments, were a young adaptable bunch and were soon indistinguishable from their Australian colleagues.

In the improvised beer garden on cool starlit evenings, Lennie would inevitably become the centre of a crowd of Britishers questioning him on all aspects of his bush pioneering experiences —a life so different from their own.

I should mention, for the non-Australian reader, that the country surrounding the Claypan, ten miles from which we were to conduct the tests, was a featureless plain of wooded country. Through this had been cut roads and tracks, along which were arrays of instruments. The following rule was written in "Welcome to the Claypan":—

When travelling from point to point keep to existing tracks or roads. Short cuts through mulga scrub (known as 'bush-bashing') can be an interesting experience but is attended with real dangers, and in any event becoming lost is a simple matter.

Interesting though it was to look for local fauna and flora, this rule had to be strictly obeyed, and it is understandable that Lennie was flooded with offers of assistance as soon as it was known that he had to make a sortie into the bush.

During the tests Lennie was given a week's leave to Adelaide, and somebody found his shopping list which, it was said, went something like:—

> new boot laces
> new tooth brush
> new car
> new shirt
> new belt

The story goes further that he had heavy duty springs fitted to his car, so that on his rare returns from the bush to Adelaide he could organize outings with a full car load of children, for yet another characteristic of Lennie is his love of children and the complete reliance parents and children place on him.

While the operation at Emu Field was being mounted, a search was made for a permanent trials site. It was essential that this site should be clear of trees, to permit unimpeded lines of sight for instrument layouts.

We received a report that a reconnaissance aircraft had spotted two such sites about 120 miles south of Emu. Dr Butement, Chief Scientist, Department of Supply, organized a search from Emu, a search heavily relying on Lennie's bush sense.

They found the area, although not without difficulties, especially when they afterwards continued southwards heading for the trans-Australian railway and encountered a range of high and almost impenetrable sandhills. Lennie will be describing this in the book.

However, a return to this area was organized almost immediately, a camp established, a runway of sorts dragged out by a length of railway line towed behind a Land Rover, and I was invited to fly down from Emu to stay at the camp for a few days and survey the area. While there, a party led by Lennie made a sortie to search for the other clear area which had been reported some hundred miles to the west. It was a four day journey through dense bush. Everybody had complete confidence in Lennie's navigational prowess and bush craft.

Back at the camp in the chosen area (which was subsequently christened Maralinga, Aborigine for "Thunder") life with Lennie was not without incident. In the bush, he had acquired a degree of proficiency in such skills as hair cutting and dentistry. I fortunately had no need of the latter but was badly in need of a trim and still have a photograph of myself sitting on a pile of car tyres with Lennie performing. The size of the clippers suggested that they were intended for sheep clipping, and Lennie completed the job in about four minutes flat. I took some comfort from the thought that I would not reappear in civilization for a week or two by which time some of the more obvious discontinuities would have smoothed out.

One evening Lennie talked to us about the Aborigines, the way they live, and the strange things they eat. Among these were Wichetty Grubs that they found in the roots of old mallee trees. As I emerged from my tent the following morning I was confronted by Lennie with a plateful of these large white squirming maggots, and I was asked how I would like them cooked. I had lost my appetite for breakfast, but Lennie ate a few with real or simulated relish.

When, three years later in 1956, I flew into Maralinga, it was then a village of gleaming aluminium, and out to the distant horizon led straight ribbons of roads and instrument lanes, the accuracy of which had the imprint of Lennie's surveys.

We then conducted our first series of tests at Maralinga. People will have different views on the purpose of this operation, but I need not dwell here on these profound and difficult questions. Whatever the purpose, they were unique, in that they drew together so many different people—Australians, Canadians, and British from all three Services and from a variety of civilian professions, skills, and crafts—and they all believed so wholeheartedly in the importance of what they were doing.

In wishing Lennie well in this latest venture and thanking him for the invitation to write this Foreword, I do not think he will mind my taking the opportunity of thanking again all those Australians who joined with us in those days and who, by their efforts, ensured the success of the work which we had been required to undertake.

W. G. PENNEY

Contents

Illustrations

Cartoons and maps by the author

1

Wanted: One Bomb Site

The huge polished desk was impressive enough on its own with its thick glass top and clean white blotting pad. You could judge its weight by the way it sank into the carpet covering the floor of the enormous office which had the blinds drawn and was so quiet you could have heard a pin drop on the desk; it would have been lost altogether if it had fallen on the carpet. The sweep hand on the silent electric clock was the only thing moving here in an atmosphere which would normally frighten the life out of anyone like me, sitting as I was in a low leather armchair before the desk with the expressionless faces of the several men present turned towards me. I'd had many pleasant encounters with most of them in the past concerning the early requirements for surveys at our rocket range at Woomera.

The day before I had been putting the finishing touches to their latest project of a new jet bombing range when I had been summoned to H.Q. of the Long Range Weapons Establishment, as it was then called, at Salisbury by an uninformative teleprinter message from the Chief Superintendent. It had merely stated that I was to come down on the old Bristol Freighter courier aircraft to see him in his office this morning, and, with the "theirs not to reason why" approach, I left what pegs I had established for instrumentation buildings on the bombing range to the care of the Department of Works and flew down to Adelaide.

The present Chief Superintendent, Harry Pritchard, was a very easy-to-get-on-with Englishman, from Cambridge. He had once given me a globe of the world from his office to help us with some spherical trigonometrical problems we had encountered at

Woomera. This was in fact his office but now he sat in another
leather armchair on one side of the desk leaving the one on the
other side to Frank O'Grady, the Chief Engineer. Frank was the
proud owner of quite a sense of humour as was shown by the
way he once pleaded with me to go and put on some old clothes
so the rest of the establishment could get on with their work.
I'd arrived on the job one day for the first time dressed in a suit
instead of khaki shorts and hobnailed boots, a fact which temporarily seemed to upset the normal smooth running of the place.
He'd had great fun in showing everyone a letter he had received
one day addressed to "The Chief *Mechanical* Engineer," pointing
out that he had not seen a spanner since he'd tightened up a nut
and bolt on his own pram.

Here again though, he sat with the others, watching me in such
a way that made me glance involuntarily down at my wrists to
ensure the handcuffs which the police sergeant at Woomera had
been recently demonstrating weren't in fact still there. I remembered only too clearly how he'd been showing me the way in
which his latest bracelets worked by literally throwing them at a
prisoner's arm to make one half of the circle spin around and
ratchet into place, and how I had been sweating as he elaborately
searched for the key he'd somehow mislaid.

There were others present in their soft understuffed leather
chairs but the one sitting at the desk who seemed to be in charge
of the situation was unknown to me. This morning was the first
time I had ever seen him. He had his elbows planted firmly apart
on the blotter with his strong-looking fingers interlaced lightly
supporting his chin, and from the sleeves of his black coat
emerged thick wrists covered with a mat of black hair. His
swarthy heavy-jowled face was topped by a shiny brown forehead
which extended all the way from his bushy black eyebrows over
to the back of his neck, which in turn came from a stalwart
pair of shoulders. He wasn't completely bald over the ears but
the eyebrows quite made up for it, overshadowing as they did

the beady black eyes which were at present fixed unwaveringly on me. I was beginning to wonder, not unnaturally, what on earth could be the matter as I searched the faces for some signs of explanation or even friendliness. But as I looked I detected signs of preoccupation, not, after all, directed wholly at me, which served to soften the atmosphere of the firing squad to a less harsh one of interrogation. Just as I had arrived at this conclusion Mr Eyebrows started to talk in a low, weighty manner. He had actually been introduced to me when I entered the office as Bill Worth, one of the chief security officers for the Commonwealth of Australia and he had already known as much about me as I did myself. "You are about to be acquainted with certain facts," he began, "which at present are known in this headquarters to no one outside this room. Furthermore," he continued with the emphasis of one used to authority, "that is the way it

3

will be remaining." I thought if someone didn't get on with it soon I'd fall completely under the spell of those hypnotic eyes. But at last it came. And it was certainly a suitably fitting climax to such a build up of atmosphere. In an even quieter tone as though the walls had sprouted ears, he concluded, "*It has been decided to detonate an atomic bomb in Australia.*"

This was something bigger than I had ever dreamed of. I partly guessed the rest—about being assigned to search for a site—before actually hearing it. From the way he was speaking and the serious tone of voice I gathered he was warning me that there was only a very limited number of people who would have to be interviewed if the project became known. Having made this point clear the Eyebrows left it now with the chief superintendent.

Alan Butement, the Chief Scientist who had his office in Melbourne, had already given instructions regarding the project. Alan had accompanied many bush-bashing camps of ours on the early extensions of the Woomera Rocket Range and was the originator of many joke sayings we still often use. Once, we were sitting around a camp fire in the sandhills discussing radar, and how flying cave dwellers use the same system in avoiding collision with the dark, dank sides of their caverns. Just at this point something whistled past one of the member's ears causing him to start violently and ask nervously what it was. The Chief Scientist, who was an authority on the subject of radar in its early development, explained carefully in a very precise English voice that all was well as it was "only one of those bats with his little radar set." Another time a member of the party who had cooked the sausages for dinner asked him how they were. "Pretty well bre(a)d," was the reply.

Apparently now however, the site required was to be in an area roughly three hundred miles from Woomera in a place where radiation would not interfere with the future missile range work. On paper it fell in an area which I knew from many expeditions to be just a sea of high sandhills covered with dense mulga scrub and nearly two hundred miles from the last cattle station home-stead in that direction. The description of the site went on to say the immediate area would need to be about five miles in diameter, and clear of sandhills so that work in progress would have the maximum accessibility and so that instrumentation could be located wherever required without topographical obstruction. This was going to be some task in this region, though one possible area sprang to mind immediately. This was a mile-long iron-hard claypan we had discovered as smooth as a billiard table, on which aeroplanes could easily be landed. It also had the advantage of being within the desired boundaries of the forthcoming event.

There was as usual a date set when the site should be ready for inspection and this was arranged to coincide with the arrival of a team of scientists from England who would be conducting an atomic bomb test at the Monte Bello islands off the north-west coast of Australia. The team was to be led by a Doctor Penney whose name was already known in connection with the nuclear physics of these tests and with whom I was soon to have many pleasant dealings. It seemed that there was time for the project with which I was then concerned, the bombing range at Woomera, to be completed. This would only take a further fortnight's surveys, and in the meantime I could plan for the new one. Vehicles could be made ready and equipment ordered in by another member whose help would be allowed as long as the main reason for it all was not divulged; he could be given to understand that it was merely an extension of the range.

I had that member already in mind; he was someone who had been with us often on hard trips and was tried and proven. I determined to ring him up before flying back to Woomera next morning to finish the bombing range.

I had a few more queries which were answered in hushed tones. Then I described the area under consideration from memory. The closest track or road of any kind was a hundred and fifty miles away through bush and sandhills, and there was no surface water for the entire distance, almost from where we were sitting at the present minute. It was not too different from what we'd been up against since the whole missile project had begun, however, and we'd do what was possible despite the odds.

After padding out of the office with the carpet engulfing the soles of my hobnailed boots, I found a telephone to have a yarn to old Bill Lloyd. He was the one I'd planned to take with me, and although he was currently employed by the Air Force I knew a brief talk to his commanding officer would be all that was required to release him. When I got him on the wire and told him who was calling I was assured of his acceptance immediately. His words were breathed with a heavy sigh of relief, "When do we go?" I replied I'd see him in an hour after the talk with the C.O. The C.O. also heaved a sigh—but this was one of resignation to the inevitable; we'd better take him straight off, he said, as it always finished up that way in the end anyhow. With a "Good on you Mick," I was transferred by the operator back to Bill who had already packed his toothbrush and said he'd come over to meet me. He was stationed only two miles away.

While sitting in my car waiting for him at the guard gate I got to thinking of the immensity of this project and what would be involved with every aspect of it. The major part of the task would be supplying water for several hundred men for a year. We'd have to make an access road out but this wouldn't be so bad, apart from all the sandhills, and food could come out on a series of planes landing on an airstrip we could make once the bulldozers were on the site. The claypan could possibly be used for a while for bringing the supplies to the immediate area, and a shorter road to the site itself could be made if need be, but whatever we did an access would have to come in from the main road. It was plain to see we'd somehow have to get a boring plant to the site for the water problem, drilling down to try our luck with the sub-artesian supplies; though, if the quality of the water was as poor as I thought, it was going to add an enormous burden to the project both in work and expense. Generally, water could be discovered at a hundred or so feet, but drilling was slow and only limited supplies could be expected. The neat bore water, barely fit for stock, could take care of the washing arrangements and most of the construction, which was after all the bulk of the consumption needed, but either way that was going to be a big part of the job.

So far we didn't even have a site but that couldn't alter the fact that the whole region was waterless—I knew this from six years of battling with it doing astronomical observations for the ground control of aerial photographs which had resulted in the first detailed maps of the area. Sometimes it would take weeks of working over the desired area almost tree by tree to pinpoint a position on the photograph which coincided with the one on the ground. As hundreds of these pictures were of nothing but a grey mass of mulga scrub it was understandable that we knew what we were up against now, especially as our area lay a further hundred miles from the extremities of these maps.

So intent was I on all the problems involved that I failed to notice the arrival of Bill who opened the door with a, "Good-day, wasn't I glad to hear from you?" from which I gathered he had not had a very interesting position at his base job. A few minutes was all it needed to arrange things; we had his truck at Woomera where most of the stores could be obtained so he would fly up with me the next day and start getting together such early supplies as we would need while we looked for an area for a "Woomera job." He didn't know and it didn't occur to him to ask where we would be going or for how long; the only thing that concerned him was how many tubes of toothpaste he should get. We had a joke that we'd measure the length of time we'd be out by the number of tubes of toothpaste.

I spent the rest of the afternoon gathering what extra instruments and calculation books I would be needing for star work as the others were still at Woomera for use on the jet range. As I worked, I couldn't help wondering what an atomic bomb looked like. The rumours that went around the troops in the army at the close of the war would ultimately be confirmed or otherwise, but somehow I thought it would be "otherwise." Some maintained it was the size of a tennis ball and others were sure it was no larger than a house brick, but there was no end to the speculation. And we might actually be seeing one! To think that for the first time the mulga country site somewhere yet to be found was to come to life in the blinding flash of an atomic explosion which was capable of razing a city was awesome enough in itself, but the knowledge that the responsibility of finding a place was mine caused me many disturbed and sleepless nights.

I had my built-up Land Rover put in the workshops for a complete overhaul by our faithful mechanics who always realized how much we relied on it in the bush, and, after booking two seats on the Woomera Bristol Freighter for the next day, I started drawing up some lists.

The next two weeks seemed to race by as I finished the surveys for the jet bombing range, and, after the buildings for the instrumentation and tracking apparatus were under way, my work there was over. Bill, with much paper work and signing of forms, got most of the stores organized. These included head gaskets, dish cloths, petrol, frying pans, and rifles, and we put them together in a corner of a shed where we could lay our hands on them in a hurry on our next pass through Woomera with our two vehicles. As far as everyone, including Bill, was concerned, we were just going on another routine reconnaissance into the bush. It was a terrible secret to have the responsibility of keeping but it was very obvious that was the way it had to remain until it was decided at very high levels to release the news. Actually it was almost a year before it was officially made known, although some people guessed pretty accurately what it was all about beforehand.

Then came the time to set off on the first stage of the work, which was to find a site for an atomic town to mushroom in the mulga within the required distance of a suitable topographical standpoint for the actual blast. It also had to be in a direction dictated by the general prevailing ground winds which in turn meant that the trend of the upper stratospheric currents had to be taken into account. It was important that the deadly radioactive fallout be carried away harmlessly into the desert. Once I got used to the initial excitement caused by the magnitude of the task, I was more than ready to get on with it, and, after another trip to Adelaide and brief talks to the powers there, we headed off to the sandhills.

Rain poured down the day we left Adelaide and by the time we arrived at Woomera late that afternoon it was so widespread that the road was made up mainly of a series of small flowing rivers. Large heavy balloon tyres for the sandhill crossings saved us time and again from being hopelessly bogged.

We struggled into Woomera covered with thick red clay, the windscreen wiper quite inadequate to cope with the sheets of liquid mud, and went in for a late tea in the mess. I was discussing with the doctor there various parts of a special first aid kit he had put together for us for the trip when the phone rang for him. He came to me minutes later to say a little child was very sick at the near-by rail siding at Pimba and her father had managed to relay the message to our hospital. It was only four miles away but the road was under water most of the way and it was still raining down in sheets. I offered to try to get through immediately —no other vehicle would have a chance of making it. The hospital could ring back for her parents to watch out for me and have the child ready.

Within the minute I was on my way on one of the most nightmarish trips I can remember for its relatively short length of eight miles return. Time and time again, while the hospital staff prepared for an emergency, I found myself moving at a snail's pace through mud to the floorboards; water cascaded across the road in the usually dry creek beds. In the pitch black of the night I had to guess where the road was for thirty yards at a time, and often with the momentum of trying to get through an unusually soft spot, the vehicle would slew about in the mud with volumes of water making the engine miss many beats. Somehow luck was with me, and I came out at the siding after what seemed like an age to be greeted by the parents waving a torch in the rain to indicate which cottage to make for. I went in with them and wrapped the pathetic little figure, white-faced in the lamp light, in a camp sheet and carried her out in my arms to install her in the passenger's seat I had cleared for the occasion. There was a radio transmitter there, so asking them to let the hospital know, I lost no time in turning around and starting back, one hand on the wheel and the other over the radio supporting her against the seat. I determined to get, if not right back, then as far as the vehicle would take us; I would have to carry her the rest of the way.

There were still two miles to go when the engine spluttered to a stop and refused to go at all. This was caused by an unusually large sheet of water swamping up over the bonnet. However, with a canvas camp sheet, the driest rag I could find and some work on the soaked distributor, it coughed back into life and we resumed our evening drive. The little girl, clutching on to my arm with a tiny wet hand, endured it all wide-eyed and pale in the glow from the headlights. At last we reached the tarred section of the streets of the village at Woomera and with a sigh of relief I drove on to the hospital where the doctor and staff were waiting at the entrance with a stretcher. After placing the girl on it and unwrapping the canvas, my part of it was over and, thanks to that cross-country vehicle, the grateful little mite was in safe hands at last.

The next day Bill and I called for his truck we had already prepared, loaded on the stores from the shed, and started off, this time in the sunlight, though the country was a quagmire.

We drove in and out of bogs all the way, pulling each other out, until we reached the last of the cattle stations we would be seeing which also meant the last of the made up "roads!" It was at this station, Mabel Creek, that the "creek" actually became a river with water in it instead of the usual dry depression. As we drove towards it, it looked as though it was going to block our way. With the recent downpours of rain it was nearly a hundred feet wide, and was flowing rapidly right across our path. It seemed as though the back country was making a final bid to save itself from an atomic attack.

Taking note of where our previous wheeltracks crossed over, what dry mulga tree to make for, and which side of it to detour, we gave it a try, first in my lighter Land Rover with the truck high and dry on the other bank. It could at least pull me back out of the "creek" should the attempt fail. I remembered the deep billabong alongside the wheeltracks to the north and knew that if I slid into that I'd really be clean out of sight. After trying it first on foot and placing a marker on the opposite bank I removed everything liable to be water damaged from the floorboards, started the engine, and slowly plunged in. As the level of the water had been above my knees when I waded through, I was not at all confident of success. As I inched forward I couldn't help thinking about the bubbling submerged exhaust outlet which would suck in water if the engine stalled, but eventually I struggled up the far bank, the level of the water coming over my boots in the cabin. The good old vehicle lumbered up the bank pouring out water like a cumbersome black walrus. Then the engine began missing violently and finally coughed its last. Fortunately, the Land Rover by this time was clear and on the dry level beyond the edge. I think disconnecting the fan belt would have helped to reduce the splashing but at least I was through. Now I could dry out the wiring so I could lend Bill at least a pound or two if he should stop mid-stream, although with the higher frame of his truck we had hoped he would have no trouble. These hopes were soon justified.

So it was we were at last on our own to battle with the odds in front of us. We would see what could be salvaged out of this country for a project as yet undreamed of in the minds of all but a handful of men.

2

The Search and Location

As we drove I got to thinking about the former owner of Mabel Creek, Alf Turner, and remembering how I had met him there six years before. The woman at the station used to make soap, forty-four gallons of it at a time out of bullock's fat and caustic soda, and she would hit me with a stirrup leather when I temporarily left "them star sums" I was doing at the time locked up in her sewing room. The homestead was of corrugated iron and this would occasionally reverberate loudly with the explosion of one of her bottles of home brew that she constantly had "on the go" for old Alf. They were real bush people and you could tell how easy going they were from the fact that there were only two water bores on his two and a half thousand square mile station because they took less looking after. One was a few hundred yards from the homestead and the other eight miles away. The rest of the sixty miles of his yard looked after itself.

The mainstay of the station was Don Tanner who became part of the place and went with the property each time it changed hands—three more times in the following twenty years—and is there yet. There was a little Aboriginal boy there, too, named Billy Brown whom I had taken on a lone trip in my open jeep half a decade before in the westerly direction I was travelling now, along wheeltracks I had made myself. I remembered we'd had a hungry time of it. I had needed one more star latitude and longitude position seventy miles into the bush to complete a map and had asked Alf if he could spare the ten-year-old piccaninny to come along for company.

Although we had been gone all day, beating through thick mulga and later into the glare of the setting sun, I still had hopes of being able to observe that night if I could locate a spot on the air photos I carried. On the way Billy had seen a bush bird we could eat and simply froze with his black hand on my knee looking in that direction. I stopped and slowly took careful aim with my rifle resting across Billy's shoulders. He sat like a statue and we were lucky enough to get it through the thick scrub without the bullet being deflected. As he was plucking the bird that night on a small claypan I had identified on the photo as a good place to fix, I had quite a lump in my throat as the poor little kiddie looked up at me with his big liquid brown eyes and uncomplainingly remarked, "We got no dinner all day."

Many years later I had casually picked up a paper in Adelaide and had read an article about a native boy, Billy Brown who had an accident with a fire. He had been badly burnt and was in the Royal Adelaide Hospital. Without loss of time I was in my car, with half a dozen children I knew at Salisbury and on my way, it being Sunday, to see him. When I got there I found he was the star boarder, and a mask was given to each one of us to wear over our faces for the visit to his ward. I wondered if he would remember me after all this time but no sooner had we entered the ward than he called out excitedly "Hello Lennie," and I saw he had several copies of his article pasted up over his bed already. When I asked him how he remembered me with my face all covered up, he said, "By golly, I bin know you from the boots!"

Now, however, Bill Lloyd and I were travelling along those same wheeltracks to look for an atomic bomb site and the larger vehicle was making much heavier going of it in the denseness of the scrub than the smaller jeep had done. We eventually came to the claypan where we had plucked the bird (all the feathers had long since blown away) and went on to an old Abo well named Tallaringa. We'd rediscovered this some years ago on another trip and confirmed the name of it in rather an unusual way. I had read an old diary of Giles, the explorer who had been guided there by a mob of blacks seventy years before on camels and had carried out a star latitude observation on it. They had given him their name for this point and when I saw it I couldn't believe that this small depression, three feet deep and ten feet in diameter, in a small clearing in the mulga was in fact the same well. I had done a sun observation at the site the day we found it and my calculations agreed with Giles' sextant figure to less than a quarter of a mile. In most cases he had only given the latitude values in his diaries, as these did not require accurate timing, but, as longitude observations need time in order to calculate them, these presented a problem. We had the advantage of radio signals now so we did not have to record as he did in one of his diaries, "A camel placed its large foot upon my watch rendering it useless, which was most vexatious as it was my last one." Apparently he usually carried a saddle bag full of them.

When we first re-located the well we'd dug down with shovels and had found the preserved, still furry bodies of several kangaroos and dingoes that had fallen in half a century before in an attempt to get water. The blacks used the well as a supply in this barren waste land and the unfortunate animals had starved to death and were finally buried.

Once at the well we pushed on slightly north of west deviating around difficult sandhill crossings in order to get our laden truck to the claypan we'd named Dingo. With all the mechanical troubles we encountered it took three days to cover this distance of eighty miles. We got there late one afternoon, and I remember how pleased we were to race over the smooth surface at eighteen m.p.h. after bush-bashing for such a long distance at five m.p.h. We settled down on the western bank of the flat clay surface— a few inches higher than its level, just in case it rained—and put up a canvas awning without any sides. On an old board table we spread our frugal meal out of the main stream of ants, opened it, halved it, smothered the mass with tomato sauce, and ate it hungrily. Then a few minutes sitting at our camp fire was all it usually took for us to be ready for our swag rolls.

Early in the morning we both worked on my Land Rover servicing it, and emptying surplus items and replacing them with petrol tins. I headed off the same morning, plunging straight into the thick scrub within a hundred yards of our bedroom. At last I would be getting to grips with what I had come for.

I planned a series of huge fifty mile equilateral triangle "recces" in every direction; after each hundred and fifty mile jaunt I returned to camp, which Bill had time to make more habitable, for more petrol and water. The extra few tins of meat only took fifteen seconds to throw on board. After each trip Bill would saunter over as I drove near the fire to roll off the huge accumulation of bits of undergrowth resembling an eagle's nest that started at the front of the bonnet and rose half-way up the windscreen. I would have to shovel this thick mat off at least three times a day in order to see out at all, though I always left the last lot in place for our morning wood in the camp. I would collect half a dozen flat tyres a day on each of these week-long excursions; both Bill and I had quite a lonely time for the next couple of months.

On one trip across a sandhill valley I spotted a rocky outcrop. I had been requested to forward any samples of fossils or minerals I found to Tom Barnes, an extremely dedicated geologist and the present Director of Mines in South Australia, so I made for it. While walking over the area, complete with my professional-looking geological hammer which had been a present from Tom, I brightened considerably when I detected a series of glazed stones at the foothill. Knowing that the seam from which these opal floaters had weathered would be on a higher level, I climbed up and found what I was looking for. As yet there was no actual colour, just glass-like potch shining in the sun. I proceeded to dig away under and over like fury with the presentation pick and soon had a large rag covered with clear glass potch. There was another rise on the same level forty feet away so I transferred my matriculation standard geology attention to that area, seeking the same strata and picking away at a great rate. Suddenly I saw some colour coming from one sample on a second rag so I discarded the hammer and grabbed it. Sure enough, bright colours emerged from its depths but my elation was short-lived when I noticed the pattern of it, one of red, orange, yellow, green, blue, then violet as I turned it in my hand in the sunlight. What a rotten thing a little education was I thought as I realized this was merely the order of colours in a spectrum from refracted sunlight.

My belt watch told me it was still before knock-off time in the city so I rigged up my radio aerial and called Ted Peppercorn who had built the set in his laboratory. I asked him to get Tom on the phone and soon I was talking via Ted to Tom in Adelaide from one of the gloomiest places imaginable; I was surrounded on all sides by a hundred and fifty miles of plain thick bush. He was quite excited when I told him about my find. I assured him that I would return in the dim distant future with my samples for him. I switched off, leaving them, by the time I'd finished, to catch their respective trams and buses to the comfort of their homes. I in turn pushed on until dark when I lay down in the dirt to sleep, full of tomato sauce and bully. I think most of Australia has been opened up on a bully beef diet.

When I got back to Bill I triumphantly showed him my samples and by the way he looked at me I gathered he thought I'd been too long in the bush. It was time for a spell after a month of this so I took him for a picnic to the opal hill only fifty miles away but only found more glass so we turned for camp. He suggested in between jolting and being thrown around in the cabin that we should go right back that night if I could find the way in the blackness. I gathered he had put his own interpretation on my word picnic so we carried on. We plunged south by the stars and by the time we cut our wheeltracks at four a.m. half a mile east of our camp I wondered if Bill perhaps wouldn't rather have camped at sundown. We spent that afternoon licking our vehicle wounds and mending flat tyres. Bill vowed it would be a long time before he would volunteer for a Beadell secret destination tour again.

Back at camp once more I realized I was getting nowhere with my search to the north so I re-examined the composite picture of the air photo mosaic I had brought. On the picture, which was rapidly becoming tattered with usage as the emulsion cracked and curled in the heat of the tin map case, I noticed an apparent disturbance in the pattern of the seemingly never-ending sandhills. I'd had my eye on this as a possible target once I decided to move my area of operations to the south. About this time a Bristol Sycamore helicopter had arrived from England crated inside a Bristol Freighter plane and after it had been assembled, Harry Pritchard, with whom I'd been constantly in touch on the radio, arranged for its use on our job. We planned over the radio that he'd come out in it with the "chopper" pilot, fitter, and special oils and greases, and we'd fly to this disturbance, hover over it, and have a look from aloft. This would surely be a change from bush-bashing, to say nothing of the excitement of the impending operation after all this time of loneliness. There was absolutely nothing to prepare in the way of a landing field, as we had the best impromptu heliport on the claypan, so, while we eagerly awaited the helicopter's arrival, we filled in the time carrying out a long-needed service on the Land Rover. There was only one helicopter in Australia at this time and it would have been naïve to imagine we could have its use here for a minute longer than was necessary.

The great morning arrived. We had smoke screens going at the estimated time of arrival to help the pilot pick out our needle-in-a-haystack camp from the air. In actual fact he literally came by road as he flew at tree-top level, following our wheeltracks from Mabel Creek, ironing out the individual twists and turns but not leaving its winding course for long at a time. Bill and I sat on the claypan to get our first-ever glimpse of a chopper. It arrived like a great silver dragonfly and virtually put on its brakes overhead to hang there, as a mosquito does while making an air recce of a good juicy expanse of skin before landing to make its jab.

Finally, in a cloud of stinging dust and sand, the helicopter gently alighted on our claypan, taxied to our camp, and came to rest in our kitchen. It was a frightening spectacle with its spinning rotors and propeller, and Bill and I hung back—we were too young to die. A sliding door opened and, instead of five green men from Mars emerging, Harry Pritchard and the rest climbed stiffly out to greet us. Everything looked so out of place here with our quiet lonely camp of the days and months before invaded in such a fantastic way. After a hurried acknowledgment of their greeting we couldn't wait any longer. We approached this uncanny spectre, half afraid that it might suddenly cough into life. All was quiet, however, as we climbed in with our hobnailed boots and bush-ragged clothes and stared at the array of controls.

The pilot showed us how you mentally line up the nose wheel and one of the off-set wheels to avoid being decapitated while the rotors are in motion when approaching the thing. Along this direction and this one only it is safe to walk upright, providing you are not ten feet tall. If you veer towards the rear you are likely to have vertically placed slots from the stabilizing rotor. However, none of the instructions prevented us from making all future approaches to it on our hands and knees, which we did until the last day before it left.

The fitters immediately started servicing it for our job, still, as far as they knew, one of the extensions of Woomera, while Harry and I scaled off bearings from the mosaic and applied magnetic declinations in preparation for our own navigation to our famous disturbance. Eventually all was ready for the take-off. The fitters, all but one who was to accompany us "just in case," stood back. Although I wasn't at all happy about this "just in case" there wasn't much I could do about it as the doors closed, the pilot placed his thumb and finger on two adjoining buttons, and the overhead rotors began to turn. From where I sat, in the front seat beside the pilot, all I could see was a great clear spherical blister of perspex reaching from overhead to almost under my "hobbs." The roof was a restful colour keeping off the sun's rays. At first I thought a pilot's job must be an easy one but later changed my mind and decided I'd prefer the role of driver on "terra firma," for as the old corny joke goes, "the more firma the less terra."

We rose an inch . . . then a foot. At the height of a man the chopper remained suspended, motionless to all outward appearances. But inside the cockpit the pilot was far from motionless—with one hand he was jiggling the stick in all directions to maintain an even keel, while with the other he was grasping a combined lever for the collective pitch of each rotor and also a twist grip throttle. At the same time both feet were working at the pedals of the stabilizing rotor for the purpose of steadying the helicopter. Then in another second the tail lifted as he eased the stick forward, twisted the throttle, and raised the collective pitch lever. We were whisked away into the sky at forty-five degrees to the ground, my black billy-can charred knuckles showing white as I gripped at something solid. It was an exhilarating experience seeing the tangled mass of scrub whizz past at 70 m.p.h. instead of 7 m.p.h. In half an hour we were dropping in on what was eventually to be our spot, although we didn't know this yet. We landed, took off, landed again, and one time we switched off the engine and hiked about in some washaways. We found nothing of geological interest—only grey billy, which has nothing to do with black billy, but is a grey shiny rock prevalent in these areas.

When we returned to our craft it seemed just a little reluctant to start. Now I was rather glad we had brought the fitter along as the engine didn't seem to be much like any we were used to. Eventually he got it firing and for the remainder of that trip the pilot kept the engine idling, only switching off the many levers involved when we were finally installed back at the Dingo Claypan camp.

Sitting around the camp fire after our evening meal, I suddenly noticed Harry's extraordinary-looking, square, box-like footwear. I couldn't make out what they were. Bill was away at the time but later he drew me aside, and, in a hushed voice filled with sympathy as if he were mentioning a deformity, he asked me what was wrong with the Chief Superintendent's feet. He'd never seen ski boots either it seemed.

Next morning it was quite cold. We all climbed into the dragonfly for a confirmation recce of other sites, although we had almost decided upon Area A as we had to call it for future radio "sked" reasons. Our final decision could only be made after I had examined it by Rover to prepare a detailed map of its topography. When the pilot put his finger and thumb on the two buttons the rotors turned and kept on turning but the engine just wouldn't start. After a quarter of an hour he grew tired, so I took over the button pressing. Still nothing happened. Three quarters of an hour later, when the built-in 24-volt batteries had slowly drained of power we all got out and assembled our two vehicles alongside the machine clear of the rotors while the fitter joined both batteries with a jumper lead and hooked it up to the helicopter electrical system. As they in turn were on the point of weakening the rotors gained in momentum and the engine coughed into life; it was ready at last. I wasn't at all confident about climbing in again, but the fitter assured us that once it was going it was all right but might not start again if switched off. This seemed to me a fairly obvious sort of statement.

During our trip that day the engine was not turned off until we were back at Dingo. I'd asked Bill to keep my Rover engine going for the purpose of charging its battery up again; this was so I could radio Ted and order the spare parts needed by the fitter.

That night with my freshly charged batteries I called Ted at

21

H.Q. but because of the poor reception we reverted to a morse key instead of the usual voice skeds. I was glad that he was such an expert in receiving morse sent out by a ham and also that I could receive his voice direct from his more powerful equipment and higher aerials. With a laborious system of my morse and his voice on two different frequencies, I managed to relay to him the fitter's request for a helicopter solenoid, some little piece of the engine which was giving all the trouble. I made up my mind there and then never to own a chopper as I wasn't quite sure what a solenoid was or how I would use it if I had one. Later on the conditions improved and we all switched to R.T. or radio telephone and heard Harry finish the sked by saying into the microphone, "Pritchard here, would you please have it out on a Bristol tomorrow?" It was only a six hundred mile flight each way for a little thing worth almost nothing but without it the machine was helpless. I could see there was going to be no doubt about our priority for this job.

The excitement of all this was almost too much for Bill and me; our claypan was rapidly turning into an airport and the population was now to rise to about a dozen. Another smoke screen, this time a chemical one, was placed on top of the helicopter to guide the Bristol in to land. The aircraft fitter came over to meet his colleague and handed him a small black object—the cause of all the fuss. The pilot from the freighter ambled over in his flying suit and stood in front of me. We both suddenly laughed and wrung each other's hand. Here, in the remoteness of central South Australia with no one else for hundreds of miles in any direction, and under these circumstances, was Len Murphy. We sat together many years ago as inky-fingered twelve year olds in short pants at the same desk in a New South Wales school and hadn't seen each other since. The only difference now was that although I was *still* in shorts he'd graduated to a silken flying suit.

In a matter of an hour the offending solenoid was replaced, and the Bristol took off on its long flight back to Adelaide. The chopper, its work finished, followed suit to be used for other useful work at Woomera. As they left, Bill and I sat alone on the claypan, watching them until they became black specks and finally vanished from sight. The population had once more shrunk from the multitudes to which it had swelled for dinner to the less hectic number of two.

Out came our tomato sauce and bully for tea, supplemented by a pudding of bananas kindly left by the crew . . . at least it would have been kind if they'd known.

3

Welcome to the Claypan

There was a great deal to be done. But we were not getting anywhere just sitting staring at an empty skyline, so we roused ourselves and prepared the Rover for a ground survey of Area A which I had yet to find. For the last few days we had gone to work by chopper instead of car but at least as a result I had prepared some compass bearings which should take me to our location across country in about twenty-five miles. I would have to mark the future turn-off to Area A, for it was important that my next trip along these tracks went off without any hitches or delays: I had gathered from a quiet conference aside with Harry that in several weeks we would be organizing an inspection of the final site by a party from the U.K. headed by Dr Penney. He was coming to Australia *en route* to the Monte Bello Islands bomb test and it was desirable to combine both trips. But the visit to us would have to be hushed up, for if it became known he'd included a remote camp in Australia the two places might be connected in people's minds, and our activities suspected. That night we ate our bananas, and with our minds full of the day's excitement and the marvels of civilization, we fell asleep in our swags.

The next day, at dawn, I ate the remaining bananas, which wouldn't have kept anyway. Then, with a wave to Bill and the more solid feel of the Rover under me once more, I headed off on my trip of indefinite length, probably about a fortnight, leaving him literally to keep the home or rather the camp fires burning and to listen to the radio each day for five minutes. With Dr Penney's visit in the offing, we were now working a little against the clock although we were at least getting somewhere.

After going five miles I pulled up, as usual without the need for brakes, broke off short as many branches on a prominent mulga tree as I had tins, and placed one on each to glitter in the sunlight and act as a signpost. It was a most effective method, but this time I wanted to make doubly sure, so I flattened a branch pointing in the direction of my projected new course with an axe and labelled it "Area A." As yet of course I didn't know how far it was to this area.

With my bearing already plotted I noted the mileage and set off again. Twenty miles further on, I came on to a travertine limestone rise. As this operation had taken nearly all day and I had a blinding headache from the glare, I camped in a small circle of the she-oaks which are often found on travertine limestone. The ground was covered by small soft needles from the trees, so realizing that I was going to have to be pretty fit in the next few days, I lay down in my camp sheet and slept off the ache across my eyes.

Morning arrived too quickly. It seemed that no sooner had I lain down than I was up again, had my swag rolled, and a billy on for a mug of cocoa—all in the one action. I sensed that I was close to what would be known as Area A. Leaving my little four poster bedroom once more to the dingoes, I plunged onwards and began a zigzagging recce. Finally, with hopes high, I came to an area about five miles across and devoid of sandhills, bordering the southern edge. It would not be a difficult area in which to move about freely, especially after some arterial roads had opened it up, and bulldozers and machinery would be coming in at some later date, probably early in the following year. I was by now quite certain that here was the site for our outback bomb trials.

Near a rocky jump-up of grey billy which overlooked a saltbush arena half a mile in diameter, I discovered a small raised flat. This would be my base from which I would carry out the daily surveys closing each traverse either to the camp or to the trash can markers I intended to leave on sticks on the way around. My idea was to use the trip speedo and compass on the Rover in conjunction with a prismatic compass, and make pages of field notes from which I could produce a preliminary map before doing the more precise work needed later. This would suffice for many future conferences behind locked doors around polished tables. Dragging in a supply of wood I made a fire to heat up a tin of meat and boil a billy for tea. I felt that everything I had been striving for since the talk with the Eyebrows was at last beginning to take shape.

Next morning I opened my eyes to see quite a sight. A huge wild dingo silhouetted against the blue sky on the jump-up with his nose in the air, stood not more than fifteen yards away from where I lay. The seasons had been reasonable with widespread rains which had filled Mabel Creek and he had lived well off the rabbits which usually thrived on the better pickings after rains. Although I knew he was mean and vicious by nature, I could not help admiring him. But there is no getting away from it; they are always on the vermin list, so I got my rifle from the Land Rover. After shooting the dingo I noticed pads from its huge paws on the ground in the dust all around my camp sheet—and it gave me an eerie feeling to picture myself lying in a deep sleep of exhaustion with this nocturnal prowler silently circling my bed. From then on I determined to sleep with my rifle loaded and cocked alongside me and to place my theodolite box at my head. I scalped the animal (this involved not only its scalp but ears, tail, and strip running down its back) and heaped white ashes from the fire on it; then I added some rocks to stop the ashes being blown about. I noticed the strip for which the Government pays a bounty measured almost five feet from tip of tail to nose.

Taking my lunch with me I set off immediately with field book and pencil for my first traverse—two miles east, five north, five west, five south, and three east back to camp, I hoped! This would still leave me some country on the outskirts for further expansion should it be needed, and judging by other projects I was almost sure it would.

At the end of each day I brought my map up to date, marking down the names of the various areas I had traversed. The first of these was the saltbush area, a suitable name in itself but one that would not help me later, in conferences, to visualize any particular area. So, instead, after carrying out a sun latitude on it at noon I named it Sun Latitude Flat. Often the traverses didn't close but I would go the full distance and adjust it all to the camp site proportionally throughout its length; of course there was nothing else there but natural features such as edge of scrub, dry water-course rise, depression, etc., but when all plotted to a suitable scale and joined up, this was what we wanted.

Every day I added a dingo scalp to the collection, bundling rocks over the ash-dried ones to stop the wedge-tailed eagles and crows grabbing them when I was away. One morning I woke on my raised ledge overlooking Sun Latitude Flat to view another but very different spectacle—one of the most amazing cloud patterns I had ever seen. Dense black clouds domed overhead abruptly terminating in an arc of perfect symmetry, shining silver in the rays of the rising sun still invisible behind the clouds, and leaving a crescent of bright blue in the southern sky which contrasted sharply with the blackness. The whole effect was quite breathtaking, and, as I stood there, unable to share the scene with anyone, I thought of another scene—this one man-made—we would be viewing from this spot perhaps in a year's time.

One night during my camp on the ledge I managed to fit in between plotting the day's work a preliminary star latitude and longitude position for the area. I realized immediately that these findings were top secret, pinpointing as they did such an unusual location in Australia so I kept the results in a canvas pouch I had especially made for my field books from a torn tent flap. I had sewn it by hand using a straightened-out sardine can opener as a needle and kangaroo tail sinews for cotton. No one would ever think of looking in there for anything but old tools, but every precaution was necessary so I kept the pouch in a locked iron box after burning the field observations and sprinkling the ashes on the most recent dingo scalp. I would need to carry out more accurate and careful observations at a later date.

Now to find a village and airstrip site. The claypan seen from the chopper on an earlier expedition was about a dozen miles or so to the west-north-west so I set off into the dense mulga out of my more open Area A to search for it.

After the allotted distance of twelve miles, there, sure enough, were some small sandhills, and as I topped the last, after half a dozen attempts with the Rover, I saw the claypan spread out before me. It was amazing the resemblance it had as seen from aloft to a stout kangaroo carrying an equally stout joey in its pouch. It was even better than Dingo and I drove down on to it, without stopping to wonder if it would support the Land Rover, ran up and down it to get an all-important speedo length, and also across it for a bearing. When siting airstrips several things need to be considered, the major one being the prevailing wind direction; however, I already knew that, whatever the bearing and the prevailing wind, this site would be used.

Next, I turned my attention to the location of a village area capable of supporting a maximum of four hundred people—this piece of information I had gleaned from the carpet conference in Adelaide. I would have to be careful to make sure the place I selected was clear of airstrip approaches, and also that it was sufficiently elevated to allow water run-off, and to catch what relief breezes can give in the heat of summer. It took three minutes to settle on the spot we ultimately used. It was a hard flat-topped rise, perhaps too hard for the poor plumbers but at least not dusty or sandy, situated a quarter of a mile south-west of the "airport"— perfect.

Arriving there, and feeling more satisfied with the way things were progressing, I jumped out of the vehicle almost on to a four foot goanna, which, after frightening the life out of me, raced for a rabbit warren several yards away at the very top of the rise. The rabbits there obviously thought along the same lines as I did. I reached for my camera as I saw the goanna emerge from a different hole from the one he'd entered and stand bow-legged staring at me. As I stared right back I stealthily approached, slowly fitting a portrait lens to the instrument at the same time. I was within four feet of him when he burst into life and retraced his steps to vanish down an adjoining hole. Sure enough he again emerged from the first opening in which direction I was already creeping. This time I had got to within three feet before he disappeared. I hastened to hole number two before he arrived and as he peered out he saw me again, and it could have been my imagination, but I'm sure I saw a look of amazement cross his face—or whatever he calls it—being by this time quite sure that the home he shared with the rabbits was haunted. Every time he looked out of an exit he saw me poised with a camera. I guessed that he hadn't seen a person before which gave me the advantage of finally being able to take a series of most unusual pictures.

But I hadn't come here just to take pictures of goannas, so I once more turned my attention to the village site. The first thing was to find a quarry site as we would be needing rubble for hard-standing areas around the village, and for building all-weather roads and concreting. I had already seen several likely-looking places for sinking water bores within easy piping distance to future overhead pressure tanks and probably a distilling plant, so this was as far as I needed to look at this stage of the town planning work.

With a revised bearing to the bomb site and a good outlet from the domestic area I drove carefully back, finally converging on to my outward wheeltracks, in order to see if the terrain would pose any problem when it came to bulldozing a main thoroughfare. I could see the country would be suitable being flat and stony, and the thick scrub would present no difficulties for a twelve-ton dozer. With a last look over the weapons area I decided to return to Dingo and radio to Harry that the plans were now ready.

At the site I came out on an escarpment overlooking Sun Latitude Flat and, eventually, to a small sharp bluff giving an excellent view of the whole area. I thought this natural grandstand would be an ideal place from which to watch the bomb go off, and although I had no idea, at this stage, what it would be like, I knew it would be worth seeing. In actual fact this was right where we did stand almost a year later for the event. We couldn't see it go off at the instant of detonation because of the glare, but we observed it after the lapse of a second and from then on.

I hadn't seen anyone for a few weeks, and neither had Bill, so I rigged up the radio at noon, assuming he was still listening daily on his receiver at that time. First I called headquarters and gave them my rather vague news about Area A, and then Bill to say I should be back at Dingo that night.

He rolled off the morning wood from the bonnet as I drove near the fire. I then went to my area, switched the engine off, and saw all the improvements he had made. It was almost like home; there were posts to hang billies and frying pans on and even a clothes line. After all, we'd been out for a long time now, about two months.

There were plans to bring in half a dozen Land Rovers for use in the future inspection by the boffins so, after servicing the vehicles, we pushed off for Woomera where we would organize the movement. The vehicles were ready and the drivers waiting there whenever we wanted them. The only way to get them to the claypan was to guide them out there. Bill's truck would act as a supply for fuel and food, and a Bristol would bring out the extras and then take the drivers back on its return trip.

The operation went without a hitch, and the Bristol landed smoothly at Dingo for the men. As the drivers were loading on their things Len Murphy, who was again flying, sat in the camp and we had a further talk about our old school days. As we walked back to his plane we decided we'd been very disrespectful to our teachers. He climbed into the cockpit beside his co-pilot who was reading a book entitled, "A guide to flying."

Everyone including Bill left, and I was alone in this howling wilderness surrounded by eight cars, six of which were brand new. Surely nowhere else but in Australia could this be happening.

The very next day I was at the transceiver early for news of the aircraft I was expecting to bring in the party. I'd heard the radio news the night before about Dr Penney being everywhere but on his way out here so I assumed the security men were doing their job well. Finally contacting the Bristol radio operator I transmitted the local wind directions and landing instructions necessary and once more settled down to wait. Soon the now familiar aircraft appeared from the usual direction and came in to land, switching off after taxiing over to my camp. I had put a pair of socks on for the occasion—no feet in them—but they looked like socks. The door opened, and out climbed the Chief Superintendent, Harry Pritchard, who wrung my hand. It was good to see a friend in these surroundings once more. He was followed by the Woomera Superintendent, Group Captain George Pither, whom I'd known since the inception of the range. Then two people emerged whom I hadn't met before but who knew me; one was Ivor Bowen the head of the United Kingdom Ministry of Supply Staff in Australia and the other a Major Gaskill. The latter was an extremely likeable man and one of the thinnest I'd seen in a long time. His hands seemed to be attached to his arms by swivel wrists and they flapped about as he talked and laughed. Then came a pair of eyebrows followed by Bill Worth, by now my firm friend. I wondered just when Dr Penney would make his appearance but Harry Pritchard informed me of the imminent arrival of a second aeroplane, a Percival Prince, carrying him and the remaining two members.

Ivor Bowen was a very English gentleman who had a sleepy

appearance and was one of the nicest people I think one could meet. I stayed with him in Melbourne at the end of the year and years later in England. I had found him in his huge office near Threadneedle Street in London and was ushered in by his pretty young secretary. Knowing him to be outwardly quite reserved she had received a start as he leapt up from his billiard table sized desk to greet me. Before she withdrew I asked her to wait to hear the story and see if she could picture it—Mr Bowen sitting in the dust in Central Australia surrounded by wild Aborigines with spears, eating a half-cooked goanna. She glanced disbelievingly at him for some verification of the story. He readily gave it, but she still admitted that she really couldn't picture it.

Soon we heard the quiet purr of the Percival Prince and after it had landed we went over to meet the passengers. With a warm greeting Alan Butement, the Chief Scientist emerged, followed by a Canadian, Doctor Solandt, who was Chairman of the Defence Science Board of Canada, as well as an M.D. Last, but certainly not least, came Dr Penney himself. I recognized him from the newspaper photographs and was introduced by Alan Butement. My first words to him were "Welcome to the clay-pan." Alan's first words to me were something to the effect that he'd never seen me wearing socks before so I promptly took them off without even removing my hobnailed boots.

With the two aircraft, and Land Rovers racing up and down alongside, the claypan was a very different place from what it had been the night before. Different people kept coming up to me asking what they should bring on the trip to Area A. Dr Penney held up a white article and asked if he'd need it, but when I discovered it was a shimmy shirt I told him not to bother. We would need any extra room we could get for petrol and water. Alan Butement had his huge rectangle of sponge rubber to tie on to his elbow to take the jolts against the door but couldn't persuade anyone else to wear one. Dr Penney saw me pumping up the pressure kerosene lamp on a box to see if it was in working order,

and, half protecting his face with his arm, he came to ask what it was. I explained as I continued pumping it was a pressure lantern, and, when I switched it on showing the white glare of the mantle among the methylated spirits preheating flame, he all but ran off saying it looked a bit risky. It struck me as funny knowing that in a few weeks he would be in Monte Bello vaporizing a destroyer with an atomic bomb. He asked me about parts of Central Australia and I described Ayers Rock with its seven mile circumference and eleven hundred foot height—all solid rock rearing up out of the flat spinifex country. He rubbed his hands together. "Sounds as if it wants cracking open," he said, with a gleam in his eye. Knowing that this was one man who was probably capable of doing just that, I hastily told him it was our most famous landmark.

Everyone seemed interested in the surroundings. A group on the claypan called me over and asked of all things, why the surface cracked into octagons instead of hexagons. I'd never actually thought about it but I tried to keep a straight face while I explained it was all to do with the lateral cohesion of the surface molecules as the colloidally suspended clay settled and dried after rain. Instead of laughing, this worldly group of top scientists thanked me profoundly and went on with their study. I hoped they knew what I was talking about because I didn't, and I noticed as I walked that ten yards away there were hexagons instead of octagons.

We required a radio sked with headquarters that afternoon, one which had been arranged with Ted to pass on information in code. As I was talking into the microphone in my Rover I had the feeling someone was watching me. I turned around and nearly dropped the instrument when I saw Bill Worth's eyebrows an inch away. He had come over to check on outgoing transmissions. Every time I switched on the radio for the entire week Bill was always standing alongside, and I began to realize just what a top security officer's job entailed. He was visibly upset when I was forced at times to revert to the morse key even though I was reading the message from a form he'd given me.

That night we gathered around my little radio receiver and listened for the report on Dr Penney's latest whereabouts. The announcer said he had flown to Melbourne and would continue on to Canberra the following day. Bill looked satisfied that his security precautions were taking shape, and Penney was interested to hear where he was supposed to be.

First thing in the morning, after something to eat prepared by the Wing Commander level air crew who had slept in the plane, we drove off into the bush along the revised and ironed out tracks I'd made on my way back to Bill from Sun Latitude Flat in Area A. We had arranged that the crew would maintain an almost constant radio vigil on both our local and Woomera frequencies.

There were four vehicles led by Harry Pritchard and me. We were followed by Major Gaskill and Bill Worth, then George Pither and Dr Solandt, with Dr Penney and Alan Butement bringing up the rear. Each kept the other in view.

Everything went as planned and before long we reached my four-poster she-oak bed room where I stopped and declared that this was where Area A commenced and from now on we would be in the potential bomb area. Everyone was eager to continue the journey so we carried on to Sun Latitude Flat, the site of my old camp. The Englishmen were wondering how I lived here on my own for that period as they were used to seeing more people.

At night we camped out of the wind in a water-worn gully as deep as the Rovers were high and listened to the radio news. The announcer began the broadcast in an agitated voice of one who has something to tell and can't get it out quickly enough. "Many Melbourne detectives were still searching the airport grounds . . ." We all looked at each other with the same thought uppermost in our minds—our campaign had gone wrong. Dr Penney's flight to

Melbourne had been announced the night before, but the reporters, naturally, had not seen him and had told the police. Bill Worth's eyebrows shot up but lowered again to shield his eyes as the announcer carried on to say, ". . . for an escaped criminal from Pentridge jail." It was a happier Bill who helped build a fire.

Dr Penney found the claypan bathroom a trifle unique

Dr Penney asked where he should sleep and I indicated a flat space beside some saltbush. We started discussing the possible night hazards of camping in the great Australian bush. When I mentioned the goannas that might amble by and lick his face, he asked what they were. I told him they resembled miniature crocodiles about three feet long but assured him they would not bite unless he grabbed at them in his sleep. During tea-time he asked what we would be having for breakfast if we were all still alive.

Next morning I took the party to my little observation bluff. Here, Major Gaskill grew very excited, flapping his hands with their swivel wrists. "If this happened to be the site," he said, indicating a part of the rise with an extra fast flap of his hands, "Maddock's stuff could go right there." This didn't mean too much to me at this stage and we moved on to the next possible site. The same thing happened. "Maddock's stuff could go right there by the tree," he flapped. I shrugged—it wasn't really important that I didn't understand what he was talking about. I would probably find out later.

The men seemed eager to see my village and airstrip site, so we drove the dozen miles involved along my new wheeltracks to a spot just short of the last sandhill still covered with brightly coloured wild flowers. I walked to the crest of the hill and pointed to the mile long natural runway. I could tell from their excitement at seeing this in relation to the weapons area that I'd just sold them a bomb site. A look over the hill, and a Rover race up and down it convinced them.

After inspecting the village hill with its haunted goanna holes on top they decided they'd had enough bush-bashing for a while, so we rigged up the aerial between the Rovers on the claypan and they asked for the Percival Prince to fly over on a bearing and distance I supplied to take us back to Dingo. I would fly over on the following day with three others and bring back the Rovers across country. While we waited we made a further tour about and I was asked what a certain track was in the dried mud on the edge of the claypan. I replied it was that of a large bird we had in the bush here called an Emu. This was followed by an enthusiastic English exclamation of "By jove, I say and all that, what an excellent short name for this site"; from then on our first bomb trial in the Outback of Australia was referred to as Emu. Twenty minutes after our radio call the Percival Prince arrived, right on lunch time.

For obvious reasons Alan in Melbourne had requested personnel be kept to a minimum for the Penney visit; this meant that each member must do several jobs. The Squadron Leader pilot flying the Prince who was doubling as our cook had been anxiously basting two chickens back in his "kitchen" at Dingo when our radio call came over. He therefore grabbed the cooked chooks from the camp oven and took off in his plane for Emu with them cradled in the lap of his flying suit. After landing, and switching off, the pilot-turned-waiter continued with his duties by stumbling out of the cockpit with a steaming bird clutched in each hand.

There are hardly any restaurants which have their kitchens twenty miles away from their dining tables, but the dinner was still hot, thanks to our "quick service" waiter. After doing full justice to this most welcome meal, we left the Rovers right where they were and climbed aboard ready for the waiter-turned-pilot to fly us back to Dingo.

We heard nothing more on the radio news and George Pither wondered what had gone wrong with the Penney publicity. Bill Worth smiled knowingly. The next day as planned the four of us drove the Rovers back; this trip, which had taken twenty minutes by air, took us all day overland.

That was the close of the inspection tour so the Bristol took off with most of the members, and the Prince took Dr Penney who gave me his boots as a present. They had been issued from an army store for his trip and he didn't know what else to do with them. He went on to the Monte Bello Islands, where Britain's own first atomic bomb was a great success, vaporizing the destroyer *Plym*. The next I heard on my little radio was that Dr Penney had now become Sir William as a result of its success. He had waved a boomerang in a conference in London which he'd got from Australia with the comment: "We should be using these in the next war."

We organized the start of the water-boring project straight-away and flew out a plant with which Tom Barnes of the Mines Dept in Adelaide once again helped, and had it under way before

37

driving to Adelaide for the last time that year. It had been a long one full of excitement and packed with activity of a physically strenuous nature so we were pleased at the prospect of a break.

On my way past the Coober Pedy opal fields I called in to see some friends of mine and found a group sitting in a circle looking very glum indeed while one or two were sitting on a coffin. I asked what was wrong and they told me old Carl Wendt over in the opposite dugout had died the previous evening and was still inside. No one, it seemed, was willing to go over and put him in the coffin which was always kept handy. I thought as someone had to go I would volunteer, so putting the coffin on the Rover bonnet I drove over to Carl's cave. I dragged the coffin inside, found some matches and a candle, and went to look for him. He wasn't in the first cave but a black tunnel led off into another one plunging deeper into the hill. There was a smell of death in the air, and it was eerie creeping on in the candle glow to find first his feet, then the rest lying back on his hessian bed, one hand grasping at an old blanket. No wonder the others hadn't wanted the job. Leaving the candle I dragged the coffin through the tunnel and placed it alongside him on the bed. The candle shadows gave the otherwise black cavern a ghastly appearance and I shuddered involuntarily as I covered his face and those staring eyes with a cloth. I wanted to get it over with quickly, so I lifted the body, placed it gently in the coffin, and covered it with the blanket. It was probably the hardest thing I'd done that year. With the lid in place I emerged into the sunlight and told the others it was done and ready for the 200 mile trip by the nearest policeman at Kingoonya, who would do the rest. As I drove away from there I thought of all the places in his seventy or so years he must have been, this was probably the most miserable to have to die in.

On arriving in Adelaide I was confronted with a top priority cablegram from England which had already gone through

Canberra, Melbourne, and Salisbury from Sir William Penney. It read "I want my boots." I showed them to Frank O'Grady nearly worn out already and said he could have what was left of them. It was a high level joke which the chiefs at Canberra were sure was a coded top secret message. A Melbourne paper wrote the story with the headlines, "What boots the Atom?"

4

Paving the Way

The new year of 1953 saw us back on the claypan. By February the bore-sinking programme was well under way, only this time at the new place recently named Emu. We had gone to Dingo on our old sandhill tracks through the scrub and collected as much of our old camp as we could heap on to the blitz truck and my Land Rover, as well as some boring equipment. The drillers, Bill, and I pressed on along the new tracks past the food can signpost, to Area A via the four-poster bedroom, and across to the claypan. The straight line route I had taken with the four Rovers had settled in my mind which way we would return in the New Year. With the drillers installed at the most likely site complete with their plant, Bill and I returned to Dingo after dropping off several old diesel drums of salty water we had collected at the old sites. These would enable them to start operations while we went for another load before withdrawing the pump rods and pump from the old cased holes at Dingo, thus cutting off our last source of supply of water. We also dismantled the engine and pump jack rig which we'd spiked to logs, and made back in haste to Emu.

There are various ways of picking a site for a water bore in this area. First by natural topography: no one would start on top of a hill. I often wonder if the person who wrote the rhyme "Jack and Jill" ever visited the Australian Backcountry. Having proceeded to the lowest part of the surrounding vicinity hoping the bedrock might follow a parallel course to the surface you search for the additional indications of dry gutters and watercourses, always keeping your mind back somewhere B.C. A point can then be tried, and if it is successful, an engine pump jack can be installed easily and the material from the bailer can run off with the least effort. This may or may not give results but mostly seems to produce something even if several tries must be made. Our observations were that water near a claypan including half a thousand mile scope in that country always gave us nearly brine. As this was a claypan job and the village was to be at hand we were quite prepared for what we ultimately got, namely water almost as salty as the sea which corroded the pipes and caked salt around taps. The pipes connected to the distilling plant filled with mineral until only a trickle came out; they had to be hammered constantly and cleared with compressed air from a pneumatic drill plant.

I did, however, after a learned talk with Tom Barnes, at that time the field geologist handling the operations, try to get very technical. I employed the method where, by using a fault line near the weapons area, a closer supply for washing future radio-active material such as clothing, boots, and undersides of vehicles would be available. It was an attempt to select the site by dis-covering the fault line, resulting in the forming of an underground dam. I found the dip of the strata and marked a point eighteen inches on the upper side of the fault where all this water might be stored, and the plant was accurately centered over my cross in the dirt. The string of tools went down, and down, and down . . . . The result was a failure that was known from then on as "The geo-logical water hole." The men insisted on sticking in the hole a signpost saying, "This is Beadell's fault," adding insult to injury by forcing me, at the point of a rifle, to paint it myself.

The two bore-sinking teams worked in shifts night and day keeping the machinery constantly on the go, while Bill and I got on with the other phases of the work. They got curious from time to time and asked in incredulous tones what anyone wanted all this water for in this country, being used to boring at stations and farms where there was good reason for their efforts. However, the old "extension of the range" theme satisfied them and they pressed on, not minding as long as their pay kept on as well.

Concerning their pay arrangements, they would put in their overtime sheets for me to sign and pass on to the Mines Dept. I was never sure which was their hardest task: filling in those forms or the drilling. Sometimes the day shift pair would argue until midnight about some point, and listening to them became our biggest source of entertainment. Old Jim Bannerman would discuss it with his snapman, the name given to the offsider of the one in charge of the plant, and the conversation would proceed as follows:

"We worked 'till eleven last Tuesday night on our shift." This came from Jim.

"No, it was 'till half past."

"No, that was Wednesday night."

"No . . . Yes."

"Yes, then Monday it was 'till ten."

"*No!*"

"No."

"Yes . . . that makes it eleven hours Monday."

They would then struggle through the higher mathematics involved in totting up the number of hours worked and at which rate.

"That makes it eighteen and a half hours."

"No."

"Yes. I worked 'er out." Silence would then prevail while he rechecked his work. "No, nineteen."

"Yes, that's right . . . no, nineteen and a half."

"No . . . Yes."

. . . and so it would go on for anything up to six hours. By this time Bill and I were so weak with laughter it was necessary to call a halt to this meeting of the "Emu Debating Society." I took to noting the times myself and acting as a president to give a casting vote, which they both seemed to find acceptable.

One night a terrific storm hit the camp as the night shift was out. Ironically enough, this was several days after striking our first successful hole, with all our labours bringing water from Dingo. Something had happened to make the team appear back in camp, before they were due, in a near panic of white-faced terror. Long before they arrived we could see their headlights through the sheets of rain with occasional silver streaks of forked lightning contrasting sharply with the usual black gloom of a camp in the mulga. When they sloshed their way in with the Rover and stumbled into the dry interior of my tent where I had a hurricane lamp burning, I first saw their pallid cheeks and noticed them both trembling as with fever, the whites of their eyes showing, and water cascading on to the dirt floor from their hats and slickers. For some time they couldn't even speak as they sought out a box and stool on which to sit while their uncontrollable shaking subsided.

I wondered what on earth had happened to put grown men into such a frenzy. Their first words were to ask me if I remembered the huge old tree alongside the plant where they hung their water bags and things while they worked. I knew it only too well as I had the plant manoeuvred in such a way that this could be of help to them as a sort of hall stand ten feet away. It was at least two feet in diameter at the base and was tall in proportion. The violence of the storm struck with such suddenness that they had run to the tree for their hats and slickers in an attempt to reach their vehicle before the rain hit. After shutting off the engine with one action of the throttle wire they had grabbed their things from the tree. No sooner had they done so than a bolt of lightning had ripped the tree apart behind them, sending it crashing in flames to the ground; fortunately it fell away from them. They had missed certain death by a few yards. The shock had set in properly by the time they got to my tent, and I think I must have become infected by their urgency as I realized that by having singled out this tree, I would have felt a certain responsibility in the event of

43

a disaster. It was true, storms of this nature were very rare but that wouldn't have helped my reactions very much.

Next morning, after a sleepless night, we pushed the vehicle to the site in the sunshine through the sheets of water and rapidly softening surface of bog holes and found the tree was in shreds; only the rain had stopped the fire from burning it completely. As it was, it presented an awe-inspiring sight.

While this work of supplying the project with its very life-blood was going on, I was free to carry out a comprehensive programme of astronomical observations for a huge grand over-all map of the whole area extending thirty miles in all directions. Barely a night went by that didn't see me dancing around my theodolite to keep pace with the tight star schedule I'd precomputed. I couldn't afford to waste a night, and I could not spare the time to be away from the instrument except to book the observations and receive time signals, mostly for three hours at a stretch. I could calculate them the next day and be out in time the following night for the next one. When the distances became greater between points I received a very welcome radio message from my old friend Ken Garden at H.Q.

Ken and I had been on many hard trips together, during which we yarned around camp fires. I learnt amazingly enough that ten years or so before he had attended the very same school in Sydney as Len Murphy and I had, and had tormented the same masters. It does seem a small world at times. He had left our H.Q. since, and being a squadron leader in the R.A.A.F. engineering group, had moved to further postings; now he had returned temporarily for this latest development. The message was short but very important for me—"Could you make use of helicopter for a week?"

In the course of several days during which a Bristol had flown in special octane fuel as well as bits and pieces peculiar to heli-copters, instead of bringing them overland, the dragonfly itself appeared. The pilot left it with the trained fitters for servicing, and we had a hurried conference concerning the programme I had planned and the number of days I could expect to retain its services. Seven, we worked out, so I resolved to do seven more remote astro fixes, one per night if I could possibly maintain the pace and keep the tremendous volume of computing abreast of the observing. A word to the fitters prepared them for this, and Jack, the pilot had us in the air mid-afternoon of the same day, complete with theodolite and tripod, chronometer, star charts, field books, stop watches, pencils, and the host of other incidentals necessary for the work in hand. I ascertained in advance that their inbuilt radio transceiver was also capable of receiving the special time signals I used.

The daily programme to make the utmost use of such an unexpected windfall followed a pattern; we arrived in daylight at the identified air photo point I'd be using for an astronomical station, and observed stars at night. In the early hours of the morning we'd fly home, the thick bush carpet passing underneath, to a bright kerosene lamp left hanging high on a tree as a final guide. I would provide Jack with a rough homing bearing which I arrived at from a preliminary calculation from my own astro fix. We could see the lamp for many miles at night, so only a rough bearing would be needed. As we flew in this eerie contraption with no wings and the chomping sound of the rotors overhead, I would start on the reductions of the observations in readiness for the morning's sums. I could be safe in saying that during these trips, I occupied the most unique computing office in Australia. The fitters would always be waiting for us to guide the last taxiing operation by torch light, whether it was two or four in the morning, and good old Bill would always greet us with a black billy of cocoa. We would loll about sleeping for the rest of the darkness, sometimes four whole hours, then the fitters would begin their refuelling and maintaining again, while Bill prepared some breakfast, Jack filled in his flying log sheets, and I dragged myself into my tent to get on with the sums. We would take off once more in time to be at another site on my old wheeltracks for a midday sun observation, complete this, and go back to camp to collate all the results. Then an early tea and off again to drop in on another site I'd chosen for barometer height comparisons on the way to the next night's astronomical station.

One afternoon as we flew I found out what would happen if Jack let go of the collective pitch lever, which he normally held in his left hand. He was opening a fresh packet of his inevitable chewing gum and with one hand on the stick holding the packet he tore off the paper with his other. The lever stayed in place for several seconds, then vibration took over and it freed itself and dropped about eight inches. The effect on the machine was immediate as it fell almost vertically for a hundred or so feet as gracefully as a house brick. Jack's left hand streaked down and pulled it back up. It was as though we had landed on a jelly and we were once again flying level. He merely grinned as he chewed faster than ever explaining that even if the engine cut out it would windmill down safely. I was unable to reply for two minutes. Another afternoon as a fresh packet appeared in his hand he asked me to fly her while he peeled off the wrappings and let go everything at once. I'm sure no one ever became a helicopter pilot in a shorter time. The slightest movement of anything did *something* so I was glad when Jack thanked me and ironed out my somewhat erratic course by taking over.

This tempo of work continued without a stop for the full week, at the end of which I was almost a wreck, both mentally and physically, having averaged only three to four hours sleep a night. Apart from the observing and computing I would often walk with an axe for half a mile through the bush from the nearest point at which we could land in the mulga to the point I'd preselected. I would then chop out a landing field for the dragonfly. I was almost glad to see the thing fly away; they were probably just as glad to go, and I suspected they wouldn't relish another such week in a hurry. Everyone had been wonderful, though, and their support had allowed me to complete one of the most urgently needed maps anywhere on any drawing board.

In the ensuing week or so everyone who thought he had an excuse would jump on the old Bristol from H.Q. and come "just to see what's what" in an important sounding tone. Then as they hurried aboard out of the flies, in good time for take-off, they would say equally as importantly, "Oh yes, now I see." I noticed that I never saw them again at the claypan. Sometimes we would stand at the door of the aircraft just inside until it was being shut then quickly hop out and slam the door. That was to trap that particular cloud of flies—flies were a constant nuisance—and air freight them back to Adelaide. However, this procedure never seemed to make any difference to the number of flies left behind which seemed, on the contrary, to be increasing almost hourly.

At this stage I wondered if I should ever live to see the end of the year, to say nothing of writing a book about it. However, we were all seeing results for our efforts, and the drilling teams had several successful water bores equipped with engines and pumps, ready for the later arrivals to connect to the camp; all were of the worst brine quality but still it was water capable of being distilled. Sample bottles of water were sent to Tom Barnes at the Mines Dept for passing on to their analyst, as also were many boxes resembling a horizontal nest of pigeon holes full of "custard" samples from labelled depths. These would be studied by the experts in Adelaide under microscopes and chemical tests, thus adding to the ever-growing number of geological maps of the surface crust of the earth in South Australia. With every government bore sunk, the same tests are carried out, and a dual use is therefore gained from each hole; so some good came from even the unsuccessful "Geological Water Hole."

All this was paving the way for the main work to follow, and in a few short weeks follow it did—with a vengeance.

5

The First Invasion

The helicopter was destined to make a third visit to Emu in a fortnight just before the arrival of the first plane-load of men. Meanwhile I had a chance to look for more possible water sites on the outskirts of Area A, and rediscover some long-lost native wells. According to Giles, whose diary indicated blackfellows had guided him there in the nineteenth century, they were about forty miles away; I was certain they had not been seen since. I was particularly interested in one named "Koonunda," for Giles, in his journal, had described it as being a thoroughly pleasant place in such a sea of desolation. He mentioned that even the Aboriginal guides accompanying them who knew the well had hesitated on some of the sand ridges to confer on its final location.

One who came with me to a remote well named Punthanna on a later excursion, had the same trouble as he would stop me on a sandhill, and climb on to the roof of the Rover to look in every direction, saying each time what seemed a very basic deduction, "It mus' be somewhere." I got him into the vicinity with a computed bearing from Giles's position of it from camel traverses and latitude observations and with an astro fix of mine seventy miles away; he did the rest. When at last we found the well and drove on to the small clearing I was not to know then that the visit was going to save the life of a pilot, as well as my own, and prevent the loss of an aeroplane some time afterwards.

We had been making a reconnaissance flight for a future road location to Emu, when a gale force wind struck us and threw the small fabric aircraft about like a feather. As the pilot battled to keep it in the air and the right way up, we were blown off course

Impending dust storm
Emu village

to the west. The plane had about a 270 mile range in its tanks and we carried a jerrycan of petrol, in case, but we'd have to land to refill. With this wilderness stretching to the far horizon in all directions that would be impossible. The pilot, though outwardly calm, looked anxiously at the fuel gauge, a glass tube showing the level, and asked where I thought we might be. As I looked down for the hundredth time for a landmark only to see the carpet of hard mulga trees, I noticed we seemed to be travelling crabwise as the gale buffeted us at will. When it eased we had no idea where we were. The gauge showed the very small amount of fuel left and I could only recall the stories of many small planes in desolate regions in Australia that had flown off into the blue and never been seen again. Strangely enough, I was by no means worried by all this as it looked like being quite an experience, provided of course we lived to tell of it.

Suddenly I made out a small rise further to the west which looked familiar to me and sure enough when I asked the pilot to go to it, I realized it was the one alongside Punthanna. Having been there with the blackfellow and driven about the clearing, I knew that it was free of crab holes or hidden ruts. The only thing was it seemed a bit short for a runway, but this was an emergency. So he circled once and skimmed over the trees which seemed to be passing the wing tips at supersonic speed as the small clearing leapt at us. In actual fact it was only the speed of a normal motor-car driving along a highway.

At the far edge of the clearing a sand bar bordered the line of mulga and as the plane dropped in, as it were, to rattle across the clearing, the well in the centre seemed to be coming at us at too fast a speed for comfort, but the small wheels of the plane came to rest, well bogged down in the sand. I knew exactly where we were at last because I had checked the latitude and longitude of it by the stars on my last visit a year ago. If you have a memory like an elephant and a skin to match, it helps you to survive in this country. We still had to dig the plane out, and

The finished airstrip on Emu Claypan
The mess was the most orderly place in camp

get it into the air again after refuelling—we hoped we had enough petrol for the mileage had been greatly increased by the wind—to take us back to our home-made strip at the camp.

We dug a groove in the sand in front of the offside wheel and another behind the near one. This was to help in our manhandling the tail in an arc using the fabric body of the plane as a lever, but first the grooves had to be meticulously lined with a cross pattern of sticks covered with salt-bush, which we tore out of the ground by hand, to take the weight. Slowly but surely our straining and pulling had taken effect and the wheels inched along their respective grooves until the aircraft was pointing in the right direction. As we had to take off in the same direction as we had landed, that is into the wind, the pilot had to taxi back past the well to the far end of the clearing. To prevent the propeller from simply pulling the top part of the plane forward in a graceful arc on to its nose before the wheels freed themselves from the sand, we did something out of the Wright Brothers' era of flying. As the pilot settled into the cockpit he asked me to swing the propeller for him and then drape myself over the tail end of the fuselage like a limp anchor chain. So with the engine idling over and loose sand gently blowing back I hurried to just in front of the rudder and flopping over the tail section like a seasick sailor I gave him a wave to indicate I was now gripping the iron tying-down loop. He slowly eased the throttle lever open to full, causing the sand to come at me like shotgun pellets. With my eyes shut tight against this I failed to notice the front wheels were slowly turning, but I soon realized we were free of the bog as we bumped slowly over the salt-bush, by then at reduced throttle. When we turned once again into the wind, he idled the motor and waved to me to climb in. The space in front, ending in ragged mulga, looked pitifully small to raise enough speed for the plane to become airborne. Also there was the thought of the seventy miles to go with what petrol we had left.

I had taken more care than ever before in plotting our new

bearing, as we couldn't afford to miss our target; the bearing was already set on the compass before I shut the door. The pilot was more worried than I as he was in charge of the plane and was not used to this sort of country; he transmitted some of his feelings to me as he advised me to strap myself in as tightly as I could, keeping my hand near the release lever. With wheel brakes held on until he had revved up to the safety limit, he glanced at me and I tried to grin to reassure him. Then he freed the wheels and waited till we were moving before hitting it to wide open. We gained speed to a point where, with the mulga leaping at us, it had to be everything or nothing in the next four seconds. The plane skimmed over the salt-bush and he kept it on the ground till the last moment. I wouldn't really care to repeat the next second as he pulled back on the stick. . . . The nose came up and we were off the ground, but still those mulga tops streaked at us. With the stick almost bent back and a slight banking, the starboard wing tip cleared the last obstruction of a taller dead tree and we were once again actually flying.

I remember giving him a pat on the shoulder as I loosened my seat harness and we flew in an uninterrupted course straight for camp. As the fuel gauge once again got to the danger level he began hoping out loud that I had provided us with a nice bearing. We landed with the gauge at zero and he returned the shoulder pat. I never saw Punthanna again.

As I recalled this frightening experience I was again looking for the native well, Koonunda, knowing that if we landed there later it would be in the helicopter and for a vastly different reason. Driving to the south-eastern extremity of Area A past Sun Latitude Flat, I struck off into the bush to where it was supposed to be, according to the camels and sun observations of Giles. I calculated I had gone forty-four miles, and it was still nowhere to be seen in that mess of sandhills; so I camped for an astro fix. From that, next day, I closed the distance to this water point and carried out a criss-cross search for it. During the afternoon of the same day I became elated as I emerged from flat-tyre-giving-mulgas and sandhills and saw a further horizon to the north than in any other direction; this indicated a sizeable depression there. After eight tries, I topped a sandhill, and there before me was a thoroughly pleasant place. I had to agree entirely with Giles's old documents. It was half a mile in diameter and smoothly carpeted with the multi-coloured wild desert flowers that had sprung up after the rain. At its centre was an extra deep depression and, with the old Rover clear of the sand at last, I made for it in haste. It was certainly man made and I crept around it for evidence of natives before finally searching the well itself. What was going to be in it and what sort of water if any? Some digging sticks and stones foreign to the immediate surface geology completed the relics; then I looked down the well.

It was as dry as the dust that had fallen in to leave it only three feet deep, and filled with roly-poly tumbleweed, which flared up and disappeared as I dropped in a lighted match. I whiled away the time until nightfall and my inevitable astro fix by digging it open with my shovel and geological hammer. I had to be careful of a cave-in—I shuddered at the thought of being buried down a hole on my own in this country, not that the prospect of being buried down one in any other country was particularly attractive. I got to the depth of the shovel handle held at arm's length above my head; my hobs were about a dozen feet below the surface. The digging was good—I had already uncovered some dingo skeletons and kangaroo skulls—so I cut down another yard to where it became moist, and finally some water seeped in. Climbing up the steps and out of the hole I waited for it to make some sort of supply while setting up the theodolite and rolling out my swag on the ground. It was covered in prickly bindi eyes which needed scraping off with a shovel first. After tying a length of plumbob string to my billy-can handle I let it down the hole and into the water. Soon I had half a billy of smelly, muddy water on the surface ready for tasting. . . . One very small sip was enough. I poured the rest of this foul liquid over the acid-soaked battery for a wash down, and started mending tyres.

From my astro fix I plotted the well exactly where Giles's camel traverse had indicated on the old map, and my latitude agreed with Giles's to about two hundred yards. I smiled as I thought of his ancient instruments, equalling results of the latest complicated ones I had, which had probably cost ten times more into the bargain. This and many other personal incidents earned the Australian explorer of the previous century my greatest admiration.

I was off again early next morning, with the star fix computed and recorded, and the tyres mended again for the day's battle. I reached Area A to find some more definite bore water locations, not that I had expected anything at Koonunda really in the first place. You learn to leave no stone unturned in everything you attempt in this sort of work, and my investigations might help some other person or project in years to come, even if only to warn them not to rely on a certain place at all. It was like building a house of knowledge in the Outback.

It was not long before the helicopter was back again, this time with my friend Ken Garden, a Mr Adams, and a Brigadier Lucas whom I had not seen as yet. Mr Adams was a heavily built Englishman, as subtle and happy a man as anyone could meet, which I discovered as soon as I took him for a drive around the area. He was straight from London, and as we drove I automatically mentioned for his interest that a wild dog had trotted past on our wheeltracks that day leaving his pad marks in the dust. They were really easily seen but he sleepily remarked in a very reserved slow English tone as he lounged all doubled up in the small space allotted with half-closed eyelids, "Really, and what colour were his eyes?" He'd obviously heard of the supernatural powers of the Abos in tracking down objects in the bush. With the straightest face I could muster I replied without hesitation, "Brown." His eyelids managed to open another millimetre and his face took on a look of incredulity. I could imagine his story to his contacts in London on his return.

Brigadier Lucas proved without doubt one of the most genuine, fair, and wonderful men I shall probably ever meet in my lifetime. Brimful of bush humour, with twinkling blue eyes and steel wire moustaches, he was well on the wrong side of sixty years old, thinnish, and tall and hard as a whip cord, but somehow he seemed to have the air of a gentle and kindly old grandfather, though I could picture him handling an erring colonel or corporal with great sternness in his army days, in actual fact he had long since retired from the military services. He had become Director of Works in Perth but was recalled to our project with his former rank to take charge of the construction programme and of the service personnel who would soon be descending upon us in force. This was our first meeting and much will be said about him later. He came to me and shook my hand with a strong grip which I liked.

It was exceptionally hot that day, and as we took off in the helicopter to visit the first inspection site, the machine found it difficult to build up sufficient air cushion in the thinner hot air to enable it to rise. Eventually we were off the ground, the pilot and I occupying the two bucket seats in front, and the three new arrivals in the bench seat at the back. I noticed the hole in the interior trim hadn't been patched yet—it was the one I had poked in one night with the theodolite tripod shoe on our previous astro programme trip. The purpose of the flight was to give the party an aerial recce of the job in hand, both for construction and administrative purposes. There were some points as yet only on paper which Mr Adams desired to check; the most important was what sort of country was in the vicinity for likely installations, so we looked at that aspect first. After examining most of the things they had in mind we went to the furthest place about thirty miles into the bush and the pilot lowered his machine to tree-top level and hovered there as we couldn't land in the heavy scrub.

When Mr Adams had seen enough he thought we could probably all go back to camp for a "nice cup of tea."

We settled back for the homeward journey but nothing happened. We just hung there without moving and from the appearance of the pilot's whiter-than-usual face, I gathered something was wrong. His jaw worked overtime at his chewing gum to keep up with his racing thoughts; he had the pitch lever pulled right up and the twist throttle right open, but the horse fly didn't respond an inch. The heat of the air higher up, being far greater owing to thermals from the ground level, failed to allow a cushion to build up. By now the mulga tips were raking at the perspex blister, and to make matters worse the overhead rotors were chomping around almost within a few feet of a dry branch from a taller tree and we all knew that one tip would be all it needed to shatter them to matchwood. I looked out the window to the rear vertical stabilizing rotor and it was also dangerously close to the tree tops.

This seemed to be getting a habit, but at least this time there was no worry about personal safety, since there were only a few yards to fall in the event of an accident, but I knew which of us would have to make the thirty or forty mile amble back for help. It was well over a hundred degrees on that day so I might even have become a trifle thirsty on the way. Then there was the salvaging of such a valuable piece of equipment. I believe the cost is roughly equivalent to the salary an average man receives over a period of twenty years' work, providing he doesn't buy anything in the meantime.

It all depended upon the next few moments, during which I considered opening the door and jumping out to lighten the load. I'm glad I didn't as later I learnt it would probably have altered the centre of gravity and toppled the thing over anyway. The pilot made a last try in a forward movement thus causing the rotors to bite into the thinned air at an inclined angle, though they still had to brush past some tree-top twigs on the way. This time he was successful; the machine rose steadily until it was clear and as we turned for camp we all looked at each other slightly wide-eyed, all except "Luke," as we were already calling the Brigadier, who was rubbing his hands together with his eyes shining at the fun of it all. The pilot's chewing had completely slowed down by the time we were ready to land in the middle of the Emu claypan. I haven't been in that helicopter since.

At last the big day arrived when the Bristol Freighter landed with the first body of men—mostly service personnel from the army engineers unit—to begin the construction works. On alighting most of them looked about them and seemed ready to leap back into the plane, but there was no returning for many of them for the next eight months. They had not been told where they were going or anything else for that matter apart from the length of time they'd be away. I leant against the front of my Rover and studied them one by one as they came to me to shake hands and ask questions. Arrangements were made there and then for them to come to my tent for haircuts.

I asked them all in turn their first impressions of my area and how they felt about it all. The first one I asked gave me his version about the situation in which he found himself by telling me which daily newspaper comic strip he was going to miss most, but he departed, consoled by the thought that if it really got him down I could draw one for him myself.

The next said he was glad to be here. As he watched volumes of his hair fall into the dust from my oil drum and flour bag barber's chair, he told me his story:

"I was a tram conductor an' one of me reglar passengers always give me a quid for 'is fare an' took all me change, so one mornin' I got sick of it an' I 'it 'im an' I got the sack. Later I went an' got a job on a station an' a shearin' shed 'and picked on me, so I 'it 'im, an' after that the station cook 'e chucked a damper at me, so I 'it 'im too, an' I got tramped. I joined the army then to get away from all these civvy coots."

I was sure plenty of those civvy coots wouldn't be sorry. The whole business was quite entertaining for me as I hadn't seen too many people for a long time. The third man seemed to have a limited vocabulary:

"I worked in a boot factory" he said, "and finish up I got to work late. The boss told me off and it was only the fourth time that week so finish up I told him to keep his old boots. Finish up he told me to finish up, so finish up I . . . well, finished up."

As the hair heaped up in the dust one of the men unfolded his family story with the resigned air of one who has long since given up all vestige of hope. He proved, I thought, to be the gem of them all:

"I come from Perth where I live with my wife, four children, and mother-in-law" Frank began in a tired voice. "But admittedly my mother-in-law doesn't stay all the time and is shared by the wife's brother and sister at their places. They have a wonderful three-way arrangement between them to look after her in turn. She goes to my brother-in-law for half the week, on to my sister-in-law for the other half," and, growing sleepier with each word, he grimly carried on with the tale, "then she stays with us for the next eight years and back to my brother-in-law."

I gave them what we usually call a survey trim, but we changed the name for this project to "Adelaide in six months trim." If the victim was a temporary visitor we adjusted the name accordingly —"Civilization in two weeks trim," and so on. One man named Merv, after seeing himself in a mirror after the six months' style said he was glad he wasn't there for a year . . .

One old, grizzled, bush truck driver was just getting over his disgust at being asked "by them white collar silky-handed gigwigs in the offices" at H.Q. before being employed for this job, whether he'd had any experience in country driving. He had pushed heavy old trucks through trackless station country in the Outback ever since he gave up his camel team in the 'twenties.

It certainly was a shock though for most as they climbed stiffly out of the plane into the searing heat to be immediately set upon by dense clouds of flies that surrounded them and crawled about under their polished glasses. And to put everyone in the right mood, the next day brought one of the most violent dust storms I had seen so far in my half year at the claypan. They had just had time to erect marquees and lines of tents with military precision, and churn up the ground in the immediate vicinity into fine cocoa-like bull dust before the storm hit us. It lasted several hours and left a trail of lacerated tents, buried personal belongings, and beaten up men. Though the visibility was down to a few yards, providing you could open your eyes at all, there was a slight lull during the space of several minutes when I could uncover my camera to record some of this. I had one of the only personal cameras in the area and all my film had to be processed and examined by the security at H.Q.

A day or so later I noticed in the small shade of a tent awning, one very rotund and purple faced Englishman, an air force squadron leader who had come to do some administrative work in his line. He was bulging over the edges of an unfortunately inadequate canvas camp chair, legs and arms spreadeagled. He wore a tremendous pair of long shorts, commonly known as Bombay bloomers, a singlet and sandals, and his skin, apart from his face, was snow white and trickling perspiration profusely. The air temperature was well over the century. His face and neck were bright crimson behind his cloud of flies, which he couldn't muster the energy to brush away, his eyes were shut, and his head pushed a dent in the flimsy wall of the tent. He had had enough and I really felt sorry for him, so went over to see if there was anything I could do for him. I was relieved to see his eyelids open a little as he replied with another question, "When . . . does . . . the . . . next . . . plane . . . come . . . along?" Then he added one drawn-out word, "Water." I was rather worried about him until the Bristol took him away on his return to London. It had been hot but I couldn't forget that helpless gasping and I doubt if he left with a very good impression of Australia.

The Australian army cooks were placid and unusually jolly compared with some other members of their vital but thankless profession. They sang as they worked in the open in the heat, with the added Fahrenheit of the stove for good measure, and one called Syd had a sort of theme song. You could hear him hour after hour, day after day, week upon week singing at the top of his voice, "Are you lonesome tonight," and after two solid months of it most of us even knew the words. The head cook, Ozzie, never failed to ask his standard question of everyone in the line for every meal also over those next two months, "Don't know if you want any of this stuff or not." Actually he was an expert and I think he did this to camouflage his superiority complex. He did his level best with whatever he had and was one who helped greatly to keep up morale. I wasn't so sure of the effect of their offsider's main song, "When I was a lad I served a term as a cat destroyer in a sausage firm." At the camp fire one night I discovered Ozzie had a sense of humour which was slowly emerging. As we went along for a mug of tea he told us in his quiet slow way that he would teach us how to make a meal out of doors. "Firstly" he said, his brown eyes twinkling when he saw we were interested, "you unscrew the hinges. . . ." He laughed at his joke and our reaction until I thought his large Adam's Apple would wear a hole in his throat.

The most enjoyable atmosphere I'd ever felt in a large camp under such uncomfortable conditions started at this early stage of the proceedings and persisted throughout the duration of the project. Still nobody really knew what it was all about but some lively discussions took place in tents after the day's work and mostly the guesses weren't far out. The army engineers were tops both as people and in their work; they entered into their labours with a will and worked at their physically strenuous tasks at top speed. They were genuinely overflowing with goodwill towards their work mates and helped each other wherever possible. Their work started almost within the hour of landing and they worked as though they'd lived there for years, some hand raking small stones from the rocky flats into heaps for the aggregate used in the abundance of concreting to be done, while others rushed from pile to pile shovelling it on to wheelbarrows to dump it in one great stockpile. Another team here threw it on to steel screens to grade it like fruit into respective sizes which were in turn collected into other barrows to be carted to the site. So far of course we had no road into the claypan apart from my wheeltracks so Bill helped with his truck which we pushed through the scrub in all areas where it was needed most. It was a pleasure and a privilege to be associated with these men.

The Brigadier, Luke, was a natural choice for a job such as this, a fact which very quickly manifested itself as he went constantly from man to man in the field talking here, helping there, advising some younger recruit, or joking at times when they all gathered briefly for a mug of tea in the scanty shade of a mulga tree. Most times Ozzie would have made some little thing for each of them from flour and jam to go with their smoke-oh and, like a devoted mother, did a lot more for them than his normal duties entailed. Luke and I quickly discovered we both did sketching for a hobby and he would always bring his water colours to me for comment and I would go to him with my cartoons. He was exceptionally good at myall trees and old petrol drums and general camp scenes.

Some younger army boys were a little uneasy at first in the presence of such a high-ranking officer but he soon knocked that out of them; at the same time he had a way of maintaining discipline if needed. When I mentioned to him one day about his being a tonic for the service personnel he replied, "Just wait till you meet McWilliams." Apparently this was a treat in store for the camp. Luke told me he used to attend country shearing shed dances in his young days in the bush, having pressed his moleskin trousers with a hot stirrup iron and having ridden anything up to thirty miles on horseback. When an official in Canberra or anywhere else along the line held up one of his orders for any reason, he would storm into my tent rubbing his hands, wearing a huge grin and showing how his blue eyes could sparkle, and state gleefully, "We've got another fight on our hands." As long as he could upset officialdom with the challenge, he never failed to get whatever anyone on the project needed in a hurry.

That was the first invasion of the former lonely claypan which Bill and I had shared for almost six months on our own, and I was so pleased to see the party was made up entirely of men of such calibre.

6

Invasion Number Two

Now was an opportune time to make a reconnaissance survey for the road we wanted to make to Emu from Mabel Creek via Tallaringa as our old wheeltracks finished there. I had never made a straight through drive to Tallaringa, but I knew it would cut about twenty-five miles off the trip, and as each supply vehicle would be required to make the return trip as well as the forward one, a saving of fifty miles would in turn mean an incredible saving of time and petrol over the months to follow. I had had this obvious course of action well in mind from the outset and was only waiting for an opportunity to put it down on the ground.

The wheeltracks to Tallaringa from Mabel Creek would be all right after a leading bulldozer had ironed out its bends, but there were still the eighty miles through virgin heavy scrub and mulga to be located in the bush. I computed a straight line bearing from my star work at Emu and Tallaringa, and, applying to it the magnetic declination for that area, wrote the answer in wax pencil on the inside of my Rover window. In these cases, my method was to drive as straight a course as the sandhills permitted. If I missed the target because of the topography, which was usually the case, I would drive over to it at the end of, in this case, eighty-eight miles, then bush-bash back on the reverse bearing but slowly, tending one way or the other, to cut the other wheeltracks. Eventually, depending on how far the sand ridges forced me off my outward course, I would merge the two, thus starting and ending the stretch right where I wanted it. It didn't really matter what happened between but the straighter the shorter. I could have laid it out with my theodolite and used pegs to follow, but this, apart from being slow would not make use of the various sand saddles and places along the ridges where an access road of this type could pass more easily.

A young air force engineer officer named Alan Woolley, who later became affectionately known for some obscure reason as "Flip the Frog" had been selected to organize the assemblage of the plant at Mabel Creek, which was at the time quite a large undertaking. As Flip was by now in the vicinity with his strings of vehicles and equipment, I pushed off on my wax-pencilled bearing on the location survey. It was going to be a hard trip fraught with the difficulties of forcing a motor vehicle through this trackless waste, and I knew already as I drove the few hundred yards across the smooth claypan from the camp, that it would also be plagued with countless flat tyres. I had advised the full-time radio operator to contact the invasion number two and tell them that I was on my way to them. As I had expected from my recces near Sun Latitude Flat, the country was very helpful for the first twenty odd miles, as there were no sandhills. I got through it in only two hours. But then it hit me with everything from sandhill mazes to some of the thickest mulga possible. The flat tyres started then and by mid-day I had two flat spares and one just gone down on the vehicle. I dragged out my well-worn tools and mended all three, pumping them up by hand, and after devouring a tin of bully beef using a cold chisel as a spoon to save washing up, I was off once more.

By late afternoon I had collected two more flats which now flopped about in the spare racks, and the country was as thick as ever. There were numerous dead "forests" of mulgas and I was never quite sure what had killed them all; but I did know some had rotted and blown over with the sharp roots standing upright from the horizontal trunk on the ground. These spots were particularly hard on tyres no matter what care I took, and generally gave three flats per "forest." I hit one such stretch about dusk and was very soon in possession of three flat tyres rendering me immobile once more.

The last one called a halt to my day's travel and by ten o'clock I was all set to go in the morning, but too tired to do anything but lie down on my swag and fall into a sound sleep. My speedo told me I'd travelled the huge distance of fifty miles from dawn to dusk, at the cost of six flat tyres and a tank full of petrol, but I was pleased to note that I'd covered ten miles more than half the distance to Tallaringa from Emu, assuming I was still roughly on line. The brakes were now useless but otherwise everything seemed all right, and the oily coating on the inside flange of the rear wheel was only due to the lost hydraulic brake fluid.

The next morning saw me on the way at first light. I had had to fit one of my mended spare tyres in place of the one which I discovered had gone down as I slept. This was very often the case, and many times as I lay on my swag in the deadly quiet of the bush I actually heard the quick hissing sound, and in those cases I would invariably force myself to replace it straightaway, more often than not mending it as well. By mid-afternoon, and with enormous satisfaction after the difficult journey I cut my old tracks leading to Dingo from Tallaringa, so followed them just one mile further on to come out right at the old well. This of course obviated the need for making part of the return journey so I thankfully carried on along my original tracks to Mabel Creek to meet up with this overland movement of men and machinery in good time.

When I finally came to them it was like meeting up with some mass evacuation with the difference that it was on its way *to* the bush instead of *from* the bush. There were four huge D8 Caterpillar bulldozers, one smaller D7 and two baby-sized D4's, two road graders, trucks with sheep's foot rollers and quarry rippers on their trays, overhead and front end loaders, Land Rovers, and almost all of them with trailers behind them. Most of the vehicles had drivers who were asleep or reading, just waiting for a road in front of them on which to drive. Owing to the heat, the open plant had rough bagging shelters tied to bush wood uprights and rails rigged over the operators; it looked rather like a mobile fowl house, but the shelters served their purpose very well. There was a water tanker among the convoy from which, with the aid of a small bucket, one could get a semblance of a shower at the end of each hot, sweaty, and dusty day.

Flip had selected a good plant operator known as Smokey, to bulldoze in front of the convoy, and it was a genial meeting for both the convoy and me, especially after I told them I had just finished a survey to shorten the distance by twenty-five miles. No one in their party of course had ever gone overland to Emu and it seemed to give the boys a more secure feeling to be able to ask, and have answered, questions about country and distance.

Meanwhile, Bill Lloyd had flown to Adelaide from Emu to take delivery of a new Land Rover fitted with radio and extra petrol tanks, for use on the job, and we were expecting him along the newly bulldozed access road. I was a little surprised he wasn't there already, but not concerned. He'd only have to wait with the convoy when he caught up anyway, at least until we got through to the claypan.

There were two air force sergeants travelling together in a Land Rover in the convoy who, as it turned out, were inseparable throughout the project—they had already gained the title of Hekyll and Jekyll. One had the added name of "Honest John." I didn't know this at first as I had never met any member of the party before that day. I had already wondered about a paper sign I had found tied to a mulga tree alongside the wheeltracks left by one of the men. It had started off with "Onest John" before the text, roughly scrawled in charcoal on the back of a cowboy book cover.

With the temperature constantly around the century mark we carried on each day, guiding Smokey on the leading bulldozer with flares from a signal pistol and sun flashes from a mirror. The blade of his machine crashing down the endless mulga scrub became as gleaming and smooth as glass with the sand from the ridges it flattened in its path. The convoy crawled along a mile or so at a time on the resulting "road" and made camp in time for the cooks to get something ready for the evening meal. One of the cooks began to remark on some internal trouble which seemed to be affecting his health but he thought he could last out until we got through to the claypan. Apart from that everyone appeared in good spirits with the adventure.

Bill was, by now, a week overdue from Adelaide, and we were rather anxious. Repeated radio calls to Salisbury confirmed that he had left on time and the fact that Woomera hadn't seen him didn't mean too much as he could easily have arrived there after dark and decided to carry on past it to camp in the bush.

I was about to ask someone to retrace our tracks in an effort to search, when a startling message came through from H.Q. The police at Port Augusta wanted confirmation as to the identity of a man who had wandered in to their station to report that a Commonwealth Land Rover he had been driving had been stolen. He said he wanted it back, but as he was dressed in bush clothes they somewhat doubted his story. They had contacted the H.Q. from which he had allegedly come and this delay had irked Bill to such an extent that we had quite a job to explain to the police that he was indeed one of our men and was on an important mission. But where was his Rover full of equipment? He was stranded with what he stood up in and they looked upon him as having no fixed place of abode, which was in this case quite correct. He had apparently stopped for a meal in Port Augusta, and on returning to the spot where he'd left his vehicle, found only a vacant space. Someone had joined a wire from a terminal on the dash to the windscreen wiper and driven off with everything. Fortunately it was found abandoned sixty miles away all intact and in good order; the robber had merely wanted to travel from one place to another the cheap way. When Bill finally pulled up beside us in a cloud of fine dust, he admitted that he had been quite worried at the time.

The track crept forward a varying distance—between five and eight miles—each day. The fitter would be out before breakfast servicing Smokey's machine for the day's work and would be all ready with the engine running for us when we got to it. Everything went smoothly past Tallaringa where everyone had a bath in a split-open petrol drum that we had left for the purpose, thereby saving our own camp water in the tanker. The drum was split vertically and opened up like a book so that the bather had to sit in one half with his feet in the other. A mile further on I came to my junction of the new wheeltracks with our original ones, and, taking the left fork which would lead us direct to the claypan, we carried on. We had all settled into a routine which was maintained, with one interruption, until we came within sight of Emu claypan. This break in the monotony began after tea time at our overnight camp with still forty miles left to go.

We had put in a hard day's work, bulldozing down scrub and sandhills and mending flat tyres which I still collected on my vehicle ahead in the bush, and we were sitting about at the end of it all as usual eating our food and enjoying the silence after listening to the screaming engines all day long. It was never long after that before we unrolled our swags and settled down bone weary for a night's sound sleep. No sooner had I lain down on this particular night than the next unforeseen adventure happened. One of the cooks appeared and urgently began shaking me with a distressed look on his face. He said to come quickly as his other cook was having what seemed to be a seizure, being doubled up in obvious great pain, and rolling about on the ground groaning in agony.

I threw off my one blanket, pulled on my still warm hobnailed boots, and hastened over to the camp fire where he usually slept. It was the cook who had been complaining on the way to the claypan; now he was incapable of talking as he hugged his knees to his chest and emitted agonized sounds. He lay first on one side for a second and then rolled over to the other, making it difficult for us to obtain any details from him. There was only one course of action and, in my exhausted state, it was certainly not an attractive one. A plane was due into the claypan the next day, and would be returning to Woomera after unloading. Could I make the forty mile trip with him in my Rover in time to put him on it, following the single set of wheeltracks through dense bush in the blackness of the night? In places the tracks would be easily seen in the headlights, but in others, where they threaded through thick salt-bush and dry sticks, they would be almost impossible to find. During daylight hours distant landmarks could be seen as a general heading and the tracks relocated at some point further along, but this would be quite a job at night. Still, this might be the saving of his life for all we knew; there was obviously something very wrong with him.

Leaving my inviting swag unrolled right where it was, I climbed back into the Rover and drove it alongside the patient. After clearing out surplus gear in the passenger's seat, we lifted him into the vehicle and quickly shut the door before he fell back out again. With a final few words to Flip, to the effect that I hoped I would be back with the party on the next day to carry on, I set off on my midnight expedition of mercy.

My passenger was still doubled up and occasionally he uttered such screams of pain that I almost doubted if I would get him there in one piece. I concentrated hard on the faint tracks, trying not to lose them for even a minute, but already they were difficult to see and we had only just started. Often checking with a torch the reverse bearing on the built-in compass, I noted that it was as it should be. I had to get through as soon as possible, for I didn't know if the plane would be early or late the next day.

After fifteen miles of frequent stops to relieve the patient from the motion of the vehicle as it crawled over dry trees and sand hummocks, charged at sandhills—this was the only way to negotiate them—and bumped on rocks, I lost sight of the tracks altogether in some taller undergrowth and drove with torch in one hand on the noted compass bearing, hoping to recut them in a hundred yards or so. After several minutes and still no sign I stopped and walked either side of the general direction with the torch, examining the ground minutely for signs. I must have walked half a mile in all with no result. I contemplated walking back along my tracks to discover if possible the point where I had gone astray, but on hearing the agonized moans from the Rover, returned to the vehicle and carried on by compass and the stars which I could see when the mulga thinned out.

Being back in the bush and off the tracks meant it was only a matter of time before the flat tyres started again as more time was spent with eye on the compass than on the ground. I didn't add to the sick man's distress by informing him we were once more bush-bashing through unknown country without help from a set of wheeltracks, and I think he was pleased at the rest he got when I became bogged on a high mound of sand eroded down from a clump of bluebush. Out came the jack and iron plate stands and shovel and I dug away in tune with his wailing, which goaded me on to faster shovelling in spite of being quite exhausted by the previous day's work. Not long after this we received another flat tyre so, much to the relief of the cook, another halt was necessary.

Actually it was another fifteen miles before I came across my tracks. They seemed to emerge miraculously from some trees. I could at last put away the torch and the compass which had done its work well, for I knew from careful speedo readings starting from Tallaringa and ending at our present camp, that we should now have only ten miles to go. The worst was over for the present and I could once more concentrate on avoiding another flat tyre. It was now past midnight. We had travelled thirty miles through that country in just under five hours of pushing the vehicle to the limit; half of the distance had been on a rocking compass card bearing to get us through. I breathed easily for the first time since having the ailing cook aboard and endeavoured to encourage him to stay with it as we were almost there. He had no idea where we were and the journey must have been a real nightmare for him in his condition. We carried on along the tracks, and came at last to the eleven miles of good going that was the approach to our old camp at Emu Claypan. I found in several rocky tableland areas that the tracks were almost invisible, but not wishing to repeat the anxiety I had felt throughout those last fifteen miles without them, I stopped the second they disappeared and made sure of them once again by torchlight before again setting off.

We drove across the familiar Claypan after forty-one miles by speedo of one of the most unpleasant night's drives I had undertaken. It was, of course, made worse by the urgent nature of the trip. It was half-past one in the morning when I stopped outside Lieutenant Keith Kennedy's tent and roused the startled army adjutant from his sleep to give him my passenger and briefly relate the story. He assured me that the cook would certainly be on the return flight of the Bristol scheduled for early on the same morning. I would receive news from the Woomera hospital later as to the seriousness of his complaint.

Although I felt like dropping on to a stretcher there and then, I realized there was time left for me to attempt the return journey to the camp to get there for breakfast and to carry on with the road without loss of time at all, so after a mug of tea and some damper and jam, and with my patient safely on a camp bed, I left the Claypan once more at two a.m. Now that there was no need to hurry I covered the distance to my eleven mile junction in almost better time, and was more careful this time to stick to my original recce survey tracks which followed better topography than I had been able to pick out in the dark several hours before. I was curious to see how I'd missed them, so took careful notice after another fifteen miles and saw where my fresh night's tracks went around a heavy belt of saltbush, whereas, before, I had ploughed through it with the shrubs closing over the ruts. In another fifteen miles I saw the glow of the cook's early morning fire as he prepared breakfast, and a little past six o'clock in the morning, I arrived at the camp almost asleep at the wheel. There would be time to go to sleep that night after another day's road making I hoped, so I rolled my swag and tied it back, unused, on the vehicle. I had travelled eighty miles that night digging myself out of bogs and changing flat tyres, and whereas they were reassured to see me again, they seemed to doubt if I'd be able to stay awake throughout the day. Some of the members of the party on arriving at the fire with plates and mugs for their meal asked where the other cook was, not knowing what drama had taken place as they slept.

Later on I heard by radio the report from the hospital where the doctor said that although it was not as drastic or urgent a complaint as a ruptured appendix, it was nevertheless an abdominal trouble which needed very prompt treatment. They were able to cope with it satisfactorily, and after a month or so of treatment and convalescing he returned, by plane this time, to the Claypan and his cooking.

In a week we were camping within a day's work of our destination, and as we sat around the camp fire I described to the party with a stick in the dust the details of what they would be seeing in a day's time and gave them a rough idea of one of their first projects. This was to start work on the construction of an all-weather airstrip along one edge of the Claypan, leaving the rest for landing on until the main built-up one was ready. It was all working out as I had visualized when I first camped on my own at Sun Latitude Flat. Everyone rolled up in their swags in a happy and genial frame of mind that night and were all up early, eager to bring this unusual and hard experience to a close.

All the bulldozers and loaders were started up and like a mob of thirsty cattle nearing a water hole kept abreast of the steel plates on the tracks, but once they saw their destination with their own eyes they literally charged across the Claypan to the camp. Smokey lowered his hydraulic blade for the last time on this trip and carried the bulldozed track to the Claypan's shore where I had one of my jam tin signposts indicating the lead out. That had come in handy a week before at two a.m. The second invasion of the Claypan had at last after much planning, preparation, and plain hard work become on this day a reality. The Claypan which had remained silent, remote, and aloof since it was formed in past geological ages had now become a hive of activity and noise, and was at last linked to the outside world for the first time by a thin bulldozed track threading its way over sandhills and through virgin scrub. This is still referred to as the Emu Road.

The boys in the camp there were just as pleased to greet the newcomers whose arrival had been imminent for so long as were the convoy to see some different faces, and there was a general livening up in the atmosphere all round.

The Bristols were still hauling in air freight daily and finally one brought the water distilling plant—an ungainly iron box arrangement with a fire compartment, gauges and pipes coming from it at all angles, and a tank receiver for the salty bore water to be processed. It was jacked up on iron water pipe rollers and man-handled on its way out of the gaping front doors of the Freighter, but as it began its path down the ramp it got a little out of control, pinning Keith Kennedy by the legs against a crate. When the load was quickly levered away from him by many willing hands, he was found to have a frightening looking dent in his leg above the knee which later turned into a blue-black bruise of enormous proportions. Being the good army officer he was, always with a mind to setting an example to his men, he dismissed the incident and carried on regardless. Apart from that, most of the unloading went without a hitch. I heard that some officials down south had had some doubts about this "still" going out to a remote camp, obviously thinking of the hill-billies in the mountains of Kentucky, but they were assured that it was only for the processing of bore water.

The army engineering major who had arrived had the nick-name of "Mountain" and I wondered at this until I met him and heard his real name. It was Alan Lowrey. He was to take a very active part in the construction programme during the months to follow and fitted well into the pleasant atmosphere surrounding this camp and project as a whole. Mountain took over the running of the still as one of his tasks and supervised its installation. Soon it was connected by pipes to old Jim's bore pump by the army plumbers, and a huge heap of chopped wood was made ready for its instant operation. The hard-working engineers erected a ten thousand gallon stock tank alongside to receive the fresh water, and the still began its work as soon as it was filled with the neat bore water. Meanwhile another team was erecting a tower upon which to build a two thousand gallon tank capable of reticulating the water to the kitchen which was also rapidly taking shape right over the haunted goanna holes. Concrete mixers were going all day long using the heaps of stones the first teams had raked from the ground for the concreting needed. I had never seen so much happen to a place in so short a time; these men certainly knew what they were doing. Being used to doing everything myself, it was a welcome change to see it all going ahead like this but it still did not leave any time for me to be standing about. Everything had to be surveyed in with pegs, and mostly I was hard pressed to keep ahead of them.

As the fresh water started flowing Mountain Lowrey began a series of graphs by which to regulate the stopping and starting of the bore engine in order to draw the maximum from the hole without "forking it" which is a term used to describe a bore that has been run dry. Soon the shower facilities were completed using the untreated bore water; spring-off taps had been installed to conserve supplies, and the whole place was equipped with concrete floors and drains. No more standing in the mud after a bucket shower.

Eventually, after the sand and tar floors had been set in lines for the tents to follow, the village hill, although not complete, was at last habitable. The great day arrived when we moved up to it from the dusty camp by the Claypan. The bulldozers filled in the fly-breeding rubbish pits and everyone collected his belongings and moved *en masse* to the new and permanent camp half a mile away; I seemed to have a lot to carry from my tent, what with boxes of computing books, table, lamp, swag, etc., so I began loading them on to my Rover alongside. Soon the Rover became invisible under the mass of items heaped on it and I just had enough room to sit in it peering out through some strategically placed cracks between the things piled on the bonnet. It took me a quarter of an hour to crawl the vehicle the short distance to my new tent in such a way that nothing fell off, and everyone cheered as the wagon slowly lumbered to the village hill camp.

That night as I was about to have a shower standing on a concrete floor for the first time that year, I took off my hobnailed boots and unthinkingly dropped them on the floor where they made a loud clatter instead of the usual soft thud. By the comment that came, "Them bluchers've got a familiar ring," I knew immediately who was in the next shower compartment. There was no mistaking old Bill's voice.

7

The Cat's Out of the Bag

Up to this time the inhabitants of the new site were the advance
working force, and, as the scientific staff were expected in the
near future, there was a tremendous amount of work to be done
to the village hill to render it completely habitable. Living and
eating arrangements had to be worked out, and the special
additions, including nearly fifty garages, required for the technical
team to carry out their work, prefabricated and lined to serve as
offices. Then there was the cipher room, remote from everything
and insulated against any change in outside temperature, to be
built for the transmission and reception of top secret coded
messages between the Claypan and the U.K. Once erected and
with the electronic equipment installed that establishment was
completely closed to all but the trained operator.

Meteorological equipment was necessary to carry out full-time
observations concentrating on the behaviour of the upper stratospheric currents. Knowledge of this was vital for deciding the
final date of the ultimate explosion; conditions had to be right
for the dangerous fall-out material to be carried away in the
desired direction. Photographic buildings for handling and
processing film, conference rooms, and administrative "orderly
rooms" were included in the programme. The main work at the
firing site was yet to come so I got busy with the survey and
initial construction of an all-weather road linking the village and
the site. So far the road was only the wheeltracks I had made
when I was on my own working from Sun Latitude Flat. Afterwards, the main quarrying and compaction of the surface was
to be organized by Flip, with Hekyll and Jekyll as foremen. So

far no one had been to Area A, or the weapons area as it would later be called, and a very easy solution to the direction of this road unexpectedly presented itself. I was about to calculate a straight line bearing between the two by means of a traverse survey and run the line of pegs by theodolite after a series of sun observations, when word came through that the helicopter was to arrive the following day. So I deferred the start of the survey until then, as I could have the helicopter hover over the point where I planned the road to enter Area A, fire a flare when in position, then merely sight it with the instrument and run the line. It was a most unusual way to initiate a road survey but it would save a week's hard work.

Soon the line of pegs was in for the bulldozers to follow; then came the grader in hot pursuit, and the initial link was made capable of carrying vehicles, while the all-weather boxed-out section in the middle of the cutting was being constructed. The red dust was feet deep after only a few vehicles had driven along it, and at the end of a day's trip to the site everyone would be coated in cocoa-like mud, a mixture of dust and sweat.

The kitchen over the haunted goanna holes was the first building to be completed at the village. Everything had to be done so hurriedly that, from then on, anyone seen using a hammer correctly by not "choking" it was made a carpenter. Luke, on a previous camp during the war, had invented a weird but highly efficient method of making toilet arrangements hygienic—"Tumbling Tommies," he called them. His method was an amazingly simple one. A forty-four gallon petrol drum was pivoted about a shaft welded lower than the centre of gravity making it top heavy. Weights were attached to the base, and a tap connected to the water supply was fitted over the open top of the drum and was adjusted to drip into it constantly. When the water level rose, the centre of gravity did likewise until the point was reached when it automatically toppled over, emptying the contents into a chute which carried them away. Once the drum was empty, the weights righted it again to repeat the operation, and the frequency of flushes depended on the adjustment of the tap. All this was outside the building and worked completely on its own, giving efficient service for the rest of the year.

Once the access road was in, the detail survey of the bomb site was top priority. I decided to carry out a complete triangulation of the whole area from the hundreds of instrumentation posts needed. Starting for one of the most precise field astronomical Latitude and Longitude observations I had ever done at my old camp at Sun Latitude Flat I measured a base line from which to originate the survey. With all this activity in the area I no longer needed to carry a rifle in my swag for the wild dogs; it was amazing to think that not long before I had had this whole country to myself. The Land Rover traverses were now helping enormously for the siting of the future trig stations, as these had to be on the highest points of the immediately surrounding country to carry out observations from, and to be seen from any point necessary. Every time I thought of the quantity of work to get through before construction could begin I would be spurred on to extra effort. The days began at first light and field work went on to dusk, when the lantern was lit and calculations commenced and continued, often until well past midnight. We had the help of two army survey corps men, known as Mick and Blue, who were concentrating on the airstrip; they helped with the base line measurements and in the erection of the trig poles—circular discs at the top of a twelve foot wooden pole, in this case painted and rigidly guyed perfectly upright over the survey mark on the ground.

Meanwhile the all-weather road was creeping out with the dozers and rippers opening up quarries or borrow pits alongside the line of pegs, for the rubble needed. This was also soon a hive of activity and the clouds of dust could be seen for miles above the line of mulgas. Each day we returned to find the village taking shape by leaps and bounds with everyone working at top pressure. I thought it would be a big project when I first entered Area A, but this was more than I could have visualized then.

The distilling plant was never idle, and it soon became evident that a second one was needed. The bore continued to hold out, but it was necessary to sink and equip others. In most cases these were successful but almost every one was as salt as the sea. The resulting distilled water, while being free from minerals, was nevertheless devoid of aeration and had an extremely unpleasant flat taste about it. We handled this problem by simply mixing some neat undistilled bore water back into it. To decide on the proportions a water-tasting committee was set up. We then mixed up a lot of mugs with labelled proportions of both and tried them out. One was found to be acceptable, but something seemed to go wrong at the first try and we nearly ruined twenty thousand gallons of fresh water. Apparently about one part in twenty worked for a cupful, but when it came to a tank it somehow didn't seem the same, and until we had reduced the level to make room for more fresh water, our tea and coffee tasted terrible. After that, the amount was adjusted, and the camp had quite reasonable drinking water for the rest of the project.

The day was fast approaching when the first plane load of scientific staff from England was due, and I began to think the mystery of "Maddock's stuff" would soon be cleared up. To give them an idea of the conditions at the Claypan which we thought might differ somewhat from those in London and Berkshire, we decided to turn out a booklet ourselves which would be handed to each one upon arrival. As well as being very informative, it would be something they could keep as a souvenir or memento of their stay here. Several of us wrote it, each adding ideas and editing, while I did the illustrations. Finally it was sent to our Salisbury H.Q. for the photographic section to produce negatives for its reproduction. I drew the cover and we called our "literary work" "Welcome to the Claypan." It showed all the scientists with long flowing beards, white coats, leggings, and tiger shooting hats emerging from their aircraft laden with golf clubs and snow shoes, with the present residents of the Claypan hiding in the saltbush watching the scene like a tribe of frightened Aboriginals. Our H.Q. publications' section bound and packaged the consignment to Emu in good time and one day Ken Garden raced over to me in his vehicle to give me a copy "hot off the press." It proved a great success.

The plane with the men aboard for whom "Welcome to the Claypan" had been designed finally arrived. I couldn't believe my eyes when I saw one did actually have a pair of snow shoes resembling large tennis rackets without the handles, and I mentioned to him our deplorable lack of snow. He was very serious as he patiently informed me that they were for strapping to his jolly old feet to walk over the sandhills more easily. Every one of these men quickly proved to be first-class and fitted in immediately with the genial, large family atmosphere of the camp, adding their own touches of British-style humour, rolling with our jibes, and giving as good as they got.

A smallish man was introduced to me as Mr Maddock. I had been dying to meet him, but all I could think of to say was "Hullo Maddock, where's your stuff?" He wondered, quite understandably, what in the world I was talking about until I explained about Gaskill. His neat little moustache seemed to quiver with mirth as he pictured what had taken place. It turned out later that Maddock's stuff was one of the most necessary loads of equipment for the project, as it consisted in part of the actual firing panel for the event.

Next, I was shaking hands with Frank Hill—one of the most pleasant men one could ever hope to meet. He resembled Maddock in build and was also to be closely associated with the maze of electronic equipment for the firing and recording of results. When everything was going wrong, he had a special saying, comprised of the one word "gloom," spoken softly and with eyes lowered. He had an absorbing hobby of collecting anything alive, both animal and vegetable, and had taken loads of botanical specimens and pickled lizards home to U.K. from his trip to Britain's first atomic test at Monte Bello. He had been honoured by having one of his discoveries named after him. I had heard about this, and asked him about it. "Oh! yes," he replied to my question, "they called an insect after me . . . gloom."

He soon had dozens of jars of preserving fluid supplied to him from London arranged on a table in his tent and asked everyone to let him have anything they came across that moved, if they could catch it in a box. His jars soon became filled with spiders, goannas, snakes, grubs, and insects, and it got to the stage when almost every time he returned to his tent there would be a strange new box in it for him. One very small cardboard box he opened when I was there was jammed tight with a coiled up live snake which reared up and was quickly entangled in his ever-present net. Alongside it was an enormous tomato sauce bottle cardboard carton. Thinking from his past recent experience that it could be nothing smaller than a baby crocodile, he took much more care in peering inside. But when he carefully raised the lid the box appeared to be empty. On closer examination by torchlight he discovered a spider, the size of a mosquito, huddled in one corner. Nevertheless, he had learnt to take more precautions and he treated all subsequent boxes with respect. The net he used was one of coiled spring steel with the fabric attached and he still laughs as he tells the story of the customs officer turning white and almost fainting as he undid his case to have this thing spring out at him. The botanical collection was also mounting as he expertly identified each piece, and dried and pressed it. Soon he had a job to move about in his tent bedroom.

Sir William Penney arrived in a separate plane. He greeted me in a loud voice, "Where's my boots and kangaroo skin?" He was to stay at the site for many months to come, so he started off with a "London in six months" haircut outside my tent. He was delighted to see the transformation to the Claypan, and had difficulty recognizing the points I had shown him during the reconnaissance.

A meeting with one of the arrivals was to have amazing repercussions six years later, although I didn't know at the time. There were so many coming at once that I couldn't remember some of them unless we had numerous contacts on the job. Although they all seemed to know me by name I knew many by sight only. Wing-Commander James Stewart from the R.A.F. was one of these. However, six years after the completion of the project I was driving a hired car in London and drew up in a maze of vehicles at Piccadilly Circus, to await the change of the traffic lights. A man drove alongside me and called out to me through his open passenger's side window in a very English voice, "I say, look here, your rear light is on and has been for some time; I thought you should know." I thanked him and replied that it must be the brake stop light which I'd look at alongside a paddock called Bedford Square I had marked on a map beside me on the car seat. I must have sounded a little Australian, for he lowered his huge pilot's issue sun glasses and exclaimed excitedly, "By jove, I think I know you old chap— at the Emu atom bomb tests in Australia six years ago." I didn't recognize him then but equally excited at hearing old familiar names in a strange country I called that it sounded pretty right. When we eventually found a space to stop we had a most animated reunion; in fact this meeting governed the whole course of the rest of my world trip. His card supplied the name which I couldn't really ask for after so friendly a conversation, and only then did I remember that we had been together at the outback trials by the Claypan.

One member of the team was a Scotsman with a very broad accent. As the day was extremely hot he made straight for the shower room, but rushed out after what seemed to me only a few seconds. He must have taken his shower, though, because the water was still cascading from his hair. I thought with all this heat and eagerness to cool off he'd be there for some time, so I remarked, "Are you getting out already?" He looked at me incredulously and explained in a serious low monotone through the water dripping off his face, "I'm oot." I could see that we'd have to find a different way of saying things.

Our new friends soon learnt our terms and used them in preference to theirs just for the novelty. They would come to my tent asking nonchalantly for a "London in six months hair cut please." They'd heard I had cut my own hair almost all my life, and asked me how I did it. I'm not sure whether many of them altogether believed my explanation until they knew me better, but I would start by asking them what they would see if they held a page of print in front of a mirror. It would be all back to front. Then if they reflected the reflection again by means of a second glass they agreed it would right itself. Seeing them wondering what all this had to do with cutting hair I would hasten to point out that if a pair of clippers were held normally as viewed in the mirror then a cut could be made exactly where desired. To see the back view of the head a second mirror would be needed, resulting in the fact that clippers held normally would be the wrong way through two reflections thus a cut tried where needed would go in the opposite direction every time. They seemed to stay with it to this point but the last part seemed to be "rather confusing, eh what!" I went on with the explanation. If the clippers were held wrongly by having the blades protruding from the opposite side of the hand, then the normal view in one mirror would be wrong, but this would be reversed in the second reflection making the wrong grip right and the cut would finally be made where it was needed. In other words you would be doing the wrong thing twice, evening the score, as well as the hair line.

All of them asked when the flies went away, as they beat at the hordes around them. I had a stock answer—"the 18th of May." Many took this literally, and some asked quite seriously if it was in the morning or afternoon of that day. That date got back to Woomera where people awaiting the trip to Emu would actually make plans with that in mind, and I heard of a conversation between two whom I had not as yet met in which one said that he understood the flies went on the afternoon of the 18th May, so he planned to arrive at the Claypan on the 19th. . . .

The Claypan was soon seething with activity as white-coated scientists complete with white sun-hats bustled about, carrying out their respective tasks. "Maddock's stuff" began to arrive and an average of four York aeroplanes loaded to the limit landed each day on the natural surface of the Claypan. An "airfield" control tower was erected over scaffolding structure on the same sandhill by the Claypan which had once been covered with coloured bush wild flowers and from which I had had my first glimpse of our future airport many months before. It was equipped with a field telephone to the camp—a feature which I soon found was to play a vital part in an emergency—and a radio capable of contacting the operator on the aircraft. The usual wind sock was in evidence, although there was now only one direction either way in which a plane could land, as the refinement of the cross strip had been eliminated by the construction party.

The places for the requirements of the weapons area based on the sketch map I had drawn on the traverses from Sun Latitude Flat, started pouring in, showing what an enormous amount of office work was needed in U.K. before the plans were put into effect on the ground. My pace of work on the trig survey increased as I saw the dozens that had to be handled, each involving much field survey and many calculations in my tent at night; we discussed the plans in order of importance in between times. Camera Posts complete with access roads, underground emplacements lined with feet-thick reinforced concrete, and the actual pinpoints for the bomb tower had to be carefully laid out and pegged in advance of the bulldozers, graders, and concrete mixers that were sometimes waiting right behind.

At last the great day arrived when the official announcement was made by Luke, at a specially called gathering. When everyone was assembled it was given out that the rumours that had been circulating were quite correct and that two atomic bombs were to be detonated at the site. The cat was out of the bag. There followed a rough overall plan for the year's programme for the general interest of all connected with the work in hand. The full co-operation of everyone on their respective jobs was needed to fulfil the schedule; there would be international repercussions if this was not met. For the benefit of any of the members of the camp who were interested in having an outline of how an atomic bomb worked—though most would probably have only a hazy idea, even then—a date was set for a night's talk in the conference shed.

Almost immediately the news was released to the world in general but those in charge had made sure the Claypan inhabitants were in possession of the facts before they appeared in the papers or were broadcast over the radio.

On the night planned for the talk the conference room was filled; almost everyone was there. A high ranking security officer, who wanted to make everything quite clear as far as the security for the project was concerned, spoke first. He stated that no private cameras were to be held by anyone unless official permission, which was hard to get, was granted, and then the film must be handed in to him for specially screened photographers at H.Q. to process; the negatives would then be examined by his section. No installation of any kind was to be photographed under any circumstances, and, whereas the outgoing mail would not be censored, nothing was to be said of the technical details. He concluded his little talk by adding that if any violation of the foregoing was traced to a member, it would mean an instant heavy fine with a possibility of up to seven years' imprisonment into the bargain.

When he sat down again an English scientist, John Tomblin, rose and told the gathering how an atomic bomb was made. He explained how a critical fissionable mass in the bomb would be electronically bombarded with one of the components forming each atom, thus giving the atom one more component than it should have. Each atom was made up of a proton and a neutron revolving around each other but this balance would be upset by the bombardment, thus flinging one of them out and into the next atom. This atom wouldn't like this state of affairs any better than his neighbour and would get rid of his surplus burden as quickly as a black ant would eject a red ant from his nest. This chain reaction would gain in progression throughout the critical mass, all in the space of a fraction of a second, and heat would be generated by the operation of each inhospitable atom.

There were countless atoms, of course, and as all this had to happen at once there would be a terrible "to do" inside the bomb which would not be capable of housing the force from the instant of bombardment. The resulting heat at its core would be warmer than the sun if that were suddenly to come to a distance of a stone's throw from the earth. On some summer days at noon we were glad it remained at over ninety million miles away, so that served as a comparison. All this energy would joggle for position to be liberated at once, adding to the confusion, and the result would be seen as an atomic explosion capable of destroying a complete town in an instant.

If, however, the mass of plutonium or uranium or whatever mass was used was not "critical," then it would generate much heat but not actually explode, and the resulting fiasco was known as a "fizzle." The critical mass was arrived at by lots of extremely complicated mathematics and the success of the event was mostly the result of obscure "sums" as Sir William Penney called them.

The site had to be prepared in such a way as to record the results and all aspects of the efficiency and effects of the weapon. By far the greater field effort was involved in this. Everyone went from the meeting slightly stunned but in possession of some of the basic elementary principles surrounding the cause and core of the work they were all engaged on.

8

The Supplies Pour In

The quantity of material at the Claypan was growing daily as the planes and convoys of trucks continued to haul in freight of all kinds. One truck coming overland with a load of cartons of tinned beetroot had temporarily become separated from the convoy and as the only rations for the trip were aboard the leading vehicle, the driver was forced to live on beetroot for breakfast, dinner, and tea until he caught up. Apparently he had been last in the line and having broken down had had to remain where he was until he remedied his trouble. It was unfortunate that this particularly driver was also the only mechanic in the entire convoy. After that incident each truck driver brought personal rations to use in such emergencies. The incident reminded me of a small bush store we visited once for supplies; on asking the shopkeeper for some meat in tins we had received his reply that although he didn't have meat he had plenty of candles. The same thing happened when we asked him for sugar; he had none of that item either but he did have have a new consignment of very good long-handled shovels. . . .

The four York aeroplanes kept arriving laden with construction material, furniture, and fresh food, and a team was occupied full time unloading them on the Claypan and farming the items out to their allotted destinations. The furniture which came from the bulk stores at Woomera was rather stereotyped, and dozens of chairs could be carried locked into each other so that they took little more than the room needed for one. We remarked on this as one load came into the camp and one English electronic expert told us that he remembered having one of them at home for six months before discovering that "*it* was *two*."

With all the talk of shortage of water, there were, strangely enough, some horse flies in evidence. Some of these were put into sample bottles by Frank Hill. Everyone was sure that they were an indication of deep cool water with reeds and bulrushes growing in profusion. Although I was able to assure them confidently that no such oasis was within many hundreds of miles of our camp I was none the less puzzled by their presence. Other insects normally associated with water came from time to time to the Claypan and they were becoming quite a topic for speculation. Some thought that they were brought up by the planes from down south, and others maintained they came up with the underground bore water in the form of unhatched eggs. With all the scientific minds on the job, the phenomenon was never definitely solved, but one thing was certain—they weren't from the area. All these seemingly small features of our life there which would normally have gone entirely unnoticed, served to bring everyone's thoughts back to ordinary, everyday things; these were as good an antidote as any to the mountainous man-made technical problems.

Early in the programme Brigadier Luke initiated us into his method of handling certain situations. He decided to show some of the new arrivals from England the conditions experienced by the overland convoys; this was to encourage the ready availability of new trucks when required. The purpose of most of his so-called practical jokes was sometimes obscure, but he could usually remind us of the results to prove his point when he needed to.

He began this particular joke by coming to me and asking simply which was the best way possible to render a vehicle capable of being hopelessly dusty during a trip, with the maximum discomfort to driver and passengers. Seeing my look of total lack of comprehension he quickly outlined his plan. By taking several of their top men on a trip overland from Woomera to Emu, ostensibly to let them see the country in between, he was going to show these Londoners what outback Australian conditions were really like. However, the whole effort and operation would be wasted, he reasoned, if they rolled into Emu in immaculate condition, so without malice of any kind, he planned to give them the most uncomfortable and unforgettable trip of their lives. Having devoted years of trial and error to the problem of eliminating or reducing to a minimum the choking bulldust drawn into a vehicle, we had merely to reverse the method to produce the worst effect. The obvious thing was to close the sides of the canopy tightly and leave the back flap rolled up. A gaping hole to the rear of the vehicle would then cause the greatest suction possible by means of the semi-vacuum created by the vehicle's forward motion. This would be quickly filled with the clouds of fine powdery red dust kicked up by the wheels, coating everything and everyone within the first hundred yards or so. As the trip was hundreds of miles I gathered he meant to turn them into a sorry sight by the time they eventually struggled into Emu—if they survived.

I gave him all the information I could supply, including the suggestion that only a very limited supply of water be carried, and he rubbed his hands as he usually did in anticipation of some exciting adventure, and climbed aboard a return plane to Woomera where John Tomblin and two others were waiting. Unfortunately for them they just happened to be in the position of being able to help our overworked and tired convoy drivers.

So it was that a week later, while we were in the mess in the period between the meal and the struggle back to our tents to continue with the sums, four apparitions appeared at the door. All that was visible were their white teeth, pink tongues, and the whites of their eyes; the rest was obscured completely by red powder, some of which was still trickling from them on to the ground. Luke had decided by dusk that evening that they all, including himself, had got the picture and being only thirty miles from Emu had come on in after dark—anything rather than sleep in those grimy swag rolls another night. Luke winked at me knowingly—he had taken my advice and the vehicle had indeed been made as uncomfortable as possible. John and the others, still unaware that anything had been planned, took it as being quite an average journey. But it had the desired effect.

Idle men thrown together in the bush tend to become discontented. But this was not the case here. Everyone was in the highest of spirits mainly because of the friendly atmosphere in the camp. Also, with the amount of work to be done, there was little time for leisure, let alone idleness. The men worked hard at their own jobs and still found time to help others carry out theirs when needed. Inevitably committees were set up to run things for the general good of our small community. Almost every day someone would arrive at my tent flap to obtain ideas and drawings for their particular group, and this was all done at night after their day's work. One such group had decided a metal badge should be struck exclusively for the members connected with our unusual project, and be on sale at a price just high enough to cover costs. A firm in Melbourne had been contacted and agreed to make it but couldn't make fewer than six hundred. After a quick assessment of the camp it was obvious that these would be all used up easily. The job of designing the badge came to me, and my work was sent off with the order. In due course the consignment was returned—a coloured replica of my drawing done in brass and enamel—and soon each had secured his prize possession depicting a British and an Australian flag crossed over an Emu, and a bomb mushroom; there was also a border with the words "Atomic Tests," and the date.

The usual camp newspaper came early in the programme and we gave it the local name which meant so much to everyone on the job—"Bulldust." There were various editors and I illustrated it by scratching at a stencil sheet with a round pointed nail; the whole thing was run off a rotary duplicator sent specially for the purpose. It proved an immediate success and all members would eagerly await their regular copies of the stapled-together sheets, giving them the only news they were to get. Luke gave his whole-hearted support to everything going on and used his position as director to obtain the equipment needed. All these activities showed the wonderful team spirit permeating the camp.

One night Luke came to me rubbing his hands as he explained his latest idea of drawing and reproducing a Christmas card for the job. It would, apart from some of the photography needed, be wholly produced at Emu—and produced in colour using a silk screen method of which idea he himself had been one of the early pioneers. I was to draw a design which would be photographed through filters, and the resulting negatives would be outlined on a silk screen. The fabric would be treated in such a way as to allow it to be still perforated only where the colour was required; the rest would be impervious for the pigment used. If a blob of colour were across the top of the screen against a blank paper, and a rubber scraper, resembling a miniature road grader, drawn down, then the porous part of the screen would allow that particular colour to be transferred through to the paper. If the process were repeated with each colour separately, a composite coloured picture would eventually be built up on the card. In our workshops at the camp, a guillotine was made out of a broken spring and section of angle iron from a tank stand. With this we would trim the finished card to the required size, thus making it a complete bush project.

I drew a design in colour depicting Sir William Penney lighting the fuse of an atomic structure with a match with the wording "Greetings from the Claypan," and at H.Q. John Stanier and his section carried out the photography, returning the various negatives to us. The production started immediately, and Luke's office took on the appearance of an artist's studio. The finished cards were stored for free distribution later in the year. A copy of an Adelaide newspaper, sent to us specially because it contained a black-and-white reproduction of our card, described it as one of the most unusual Christmas cards ever produced.

Meanwhile a chubby new arrival was proudly introduced to the camp by Luke as the famous "Chinny McWilliams." Luke and he had been together in the army and the relationship had proved a particularly lively one resulting in Luke's decision to secure McWilliams's services, if, for no other reason, than to boost and keep the morale at its highest at all times. Actually Chinny, whose nickname came from his rather solid-looking lower jaw, was an engineer quite conversant and expert with the use of explosives, a feature which was later to liven up the camp considerably. Soon he became a favourite with everyone, as his bubbling-over nature came unsuppressed to the fore with a liveliness that would be hard to match.

A fifty-two ton Centurion tank was scheduled to arrive on the job next, so that the effect of the bomb blast on it could be studied. Apparently it could have been placed in a position where it would have been completely vaporized, but, instead, it was put in a place where it was hoped there would be something left to study. It was to be brought as far as possible on a low-loader, then driven over the sandhills. I pegged out the spot for its destination near the bomb and went to meet it in order to guide it across country by the shortest route to its possible graveyard. At first glance it resembled a huge iron structure covered with what looked like a bonfire: sticks and branches broken off the mulgas had collected on it and had been ignited by the exposed exhaust pipes from the screaming engines. It didn't seem to worry the crew who occasionally shovelled the fire off, and it certainly didn't burn the great steel monster. When we met along the only road we had made to Emu we all stopped for a mug of tea boiled on top of the tank and I had a look inside it. The windscreen was thicker than it was long or wide and the controls were more like those in an airliner than in a ground vehicle; I wondered what chance it would have of negotiating the high sand ridges involved to get it straight to its resting place. My doubts were quickly dispelled, however, as I saw it climb up the hills mowing down the largest of the mulga trees in its path as if they were matchwood and lumbering after my little Land Rover like a bull in a Spanish Arena. Soon it had covered the distance and was manoeuvred into place, side on to the future bomb blast.

When I returned to the Claypan and went into the office of the ones concerned with this part of the test, I was shocked to see a person with his head slumped over a desk, as motionless as a dead man. He was wearing a coat, gloves, and rubber boots. As I carefully touched him one arm fell to his side and just hung there. I was growing seriously alarmed, when a voice from behind the door asked me cheerfully if I'd met Cecil. Cecil was made of straw jammed into a sacking figure of a man and dressed over the hessian to resemble closely an average-sized tank driver. He was to be seated at the controls when the bomb went off so that the scientists could see how the tank would protect its crew in the event of an atomic attack. Relieved, I explained that the Centurion was now in place to be set up as required.

As a small variation and break in the work, a sports morning was organized, the highlight of which was to be the "old codgers' race." The only ones eligible were those over the age of fifty, but because of the young average age of the camp, this figure had to be reduced to forty in order to get enough competitors. Hekyll and Jekyll turned up complete with headbands made of Emu feathers and blackened faces, while Ken Garden wore his best red polka-dotted shortie pyjamas. Chinny McWilliams came with a supply of cabbages and a hurricane lamp in case he was still trying to finish the course after nightfall, and an old Scottish handyman brought a loaf of bread and a tin of jam for his late supper on the road. Allan the security officer acted as bookmaker for the race; a pillow attached to his front turned him quite successfully into a stoutish man; he had a survey bag hanging from his neck on his "corporation" with his name—"Ike Kopthelot"—clearly printed on the attached card. Everyone entered into the fun of the thing whole-heartedly as was usual in this camp, and Chinny even lit the half plug of gelignite as a starting shot. They all finished the long course from the haunted goanna hole kitchen to the end of the Claypan and back . . . then found they couldn't move properly for days. The old Scotsman won and, as a prize, had his washing done for him by the others for a week.

A plan arrived showing where over a thousand small instruments were to be accurately placed—radially to the future bomb tower. This was to keep me very busy until the pegs were in. Before starting, I resolved to build a two mile fence to keep off the traffic, and sought the professional assistance of a former dairy farmer. Each post hole had to be sunk with a compressor unit attached to a pneumatic drill as the ground was composed of solid iron-hard travertine limestone. The instruments to be installed were in the form of "velocity of shock" blast switches, toothpaste tubes to measure blast, heat indicators, and numerous others for showing the progressive deterioration of the effects of the bomb in general as the distance from its core became greater. A firm in England had been asked to supply thousands of toothpaste tubes, minus—to their surprise—the paste. These were to be placed in slotted baffle plates in groups directed at the bomb; the blast would destroy the nearer ones, flatten those further out, and only slightly dent the extreme groups. The rate of deterioration would be given later by measuring the volume of the misshapen tubes.

One of the dozens of specialized cameras for recording the ultimate event arrived, and I was told it was capable of taking photographs at the rate of half a million frames per second. Later I thought I must have heard incorrectly, but the figure was in fact five hundred thousand pictures a second. Of course, sufficient length of film for such a number was not capable of being stored in the instrument, so less than a hundred would be taken at that rate. Allowing a decimal of a second to warm up to that, and another for the film to flick past, the whole thing would be in operation for less than a second. This required a precise timing device that electronically triggered the camera to start when the fireball was to form. We hoped to observe the disintegration of the tower on a subsequent showing of the film. This was just another item to be connected to the maze of wiring involved. The whole thing was to be actuated by the pressing of a single red button.

Maddock's stuff, involving this button and firing panel, was arriving constantly, and I agreed with Gaskill that Maddock would indeed want the pick of the forward area to store it. Boxes and crates of all sizes and shapes were already heaped up near his allotted area.

The firing control seemed a relatively simple one. It consisted of several clocks, three buttons, some cathode ray tubes, a board covered with lights, and a row of key holes ending with a large black master key. These were for "personnel keys" to be in the possession of men who had jobs to do at the last minute near the bomb tower, and the master key was to be kept by the people actually arming the weapon. Unless every one of the keys was inserted and switched on, and the master key installed, the firing button was useless.

The three buttons each had self-explanatory labels under them—"start," "delay," and "disarm." When a so-called firing button is pressed it really initiates a pre-planned electronic programme bringing into play recording instruments at various stages throughout the countdown. The rows of lights show if there is any malfunction of any item of equipment, pinpointing which one, and giving an indication if a remedy can be effected quickly using the delay button, or whether a complete disarming operation is necessary. The clocks were divided separately, one into four minutes, as in our case at Emu, the next into one minute, and another into seconds with the one hand of each moving at appropriately different speeds. As each minute came up, the next row of lights would be lit and if one was missing it showed which instrument was not working. When the third minute came along the observers, Maddock and Frank Hill, would direct their attention to the next dial, and so on, so that they would be able to give the verbal countdown of the last few seconds over their desk microphone to be relayed to loud speakers placed so that everyone could hear.

To me it was an amazing piece of equipment but the ones who developed and worked to perfect it looked upon it as being just another phase of the programme. The weird patterns shown on the cathode ray tubes told a complete story to those concerned, but to me they resembled lines of stones at an Aboriginal corroboree ground.

The two army survey corps men, Mick and Blue worked wonderfully well together. Mick had developed an attachment to a dog which arrived on one of the Yorks. He called it Pat and was never seen without it beside him as he worked or slept; they went together under the name of Pat and Mick after the two Irishmen described in so many old and hackneyed jokes. Mick grew a huge black bushy moustache and one day as he was painting a trig pole, Blue remarked on his likeness to Adolf Hitler. However, Mick quickly suppressed that in case it got around as a nickname. Both men were always ready and willing to help me when the pressure was on and when I needed six hands at once as in chaining lines. But these occasions were rare as it was possible to lay out most of the work from my original trig survey which was proving invaluable.

Even the Army and the Navy were involved. Several pieces of battleships were hauled in to be reassembled alongside the instrument lanes. The sight of a section of superstructure of a ship sitting out here in the desert looked strange but the Navy wished to record the effect of an atomic explosion on their ships.

Army units brought along samples of all types of ammunition and high explosives to place about at strategic points and see what could happen to them. Catering units came along with cases of tinned rations to have tested after the event, and these added to the rapidly growing array of test pieces all of which had been freighted to the site from hundreds of miles down south. The work seemed insurmountable and appeared to grow in intensity as the days and weeks passed. There was no apparent hope of getting ahead of it, but it just had to be done before the trial's date and that was that. A full-time carpenter's shop was fitted out with mechanical saws, and there were tradesmen who coped with special requirements as far as woodwork was concerned. The overworked York aircraft and Bristol Freighters kept coming, unloading, and returning for more, still using the natural unmade surface of the original claypan, as the all-weather strip alongside was not yet complete.

Everything was progressing as I had anticipated and planned in my mind on my first visit to Area A. I had begun to treat the whole thing more as an interesting hobby than as a job. This attitude was probably a fortunate one for without it I doubt if I could have carried out my part of the proceedings. The constant traffic on the "helicopter" road to the site was already corrugating the formed surface, and a grader was occupied almost full time in keeping it in order, not only for comfort and the reduction to a minimum of the wear and tear on the vehicles, but also for the preservation of the delicate and valuable equipment carried.

The Air Force needed its share of effects of atomic blasts and shock waves to aeroplanes, so resurrected half a dozen old Mustang single-seater fighters from a depot in New South Wales, and their fitters rendered them capable of flying again. There was something wrong with most of them—anything from faulty hydraulic lines for brakes to cracked duralumin skin on the wings—but half a dozen pilots volunteered to fly them to Emu. One day they began arriving and as each landed we watched with bated breath for any signs of disaster. Some came in without

Sir William Penney watches his medal being made

incident, but one of them came in at a terrific speed as the hydraulically operated air-brake flaps failed to respond. At last it came to rest after using the complete length of the Claypan, in the sandy section on the over-run. It had to be towed out of the sand before it could be taxied to a spot on the Claypan out of the way. Another landed at a normal speed with flaps down but didn't seem to have any brakes and rolled on and on till it, too, came to rest in the sand. The worst landing was the last one. This particular aircraft had lost a good percentage of control on its ailerons and bounced from one wheel to the other until it righted itself for the final taxiing run to its resting place. The intrepid pilots stayed overnight and returned on one of the Yorks which had been fitted out with six seats for the occasion.

The problem now was to transport the planes the dozen or so miles to their final graveyard near the bomb. As their under-carriages were not up to such a long towing operation, a sledge arrangement was made up in the workshops in the form of a triangle, the angles of which were fitted with steel shoes to take a wheel each. The frame was made of heavy iron and included tying-down rings welded where needed and chains attached for towing. The road out had been specially made wide enough to accommodate the wing span, and as each plane was rolled on to the sled and tied down, a small D4 bulldozer towed it out to its allotted position. They looked a queer sight as they glided along behind the clouds of dust thrown up by the dozer, with their propellers stationary. Some were directed at the bomb site, others sat side-on or tail-on, and two were behind bulldozed protective mounds of varied thicknesses and heights.

The appearance of my old Sun Latitude Flat was something I could never have visualized, with battleships minus water, hundreds of toothpaste tubes minus toothpaste, and aeroplanes minus aerodromes. The enormity of the programme was fast becoming apparent—out of all proportion to what I could have foreseen—and this was only the beginning . . . .

9

Plain Hard Yacca

Ernie May was the one responsible for keeping everyone at it full speed and soon he became generally known as "the Whip." He was an army engineer's Sergeant-Major operating on many projects as the service version of a civilian foreman and had been very knowledgeable about big construction projects even before he joined the army. With such a huge job to do here where he was also the main field contact with the men on the job, he was as hard as hobnails but fair and straight-forward at the same time. Ernie was never to be seen without rolls of plans under his arm. Anybody he saw leaning on a shovel or resting on wheelbarrow handles would be told to "Go on, move about there." When the date came around to the first of May everyone unanimously agreed that they would be glad to see the last of May, but he was nevertheless respected for his ability and also for the way in which he whole-heartedly entered into jokes about himself off the job. After work he was a grand mate to have.

I knew what a burden he had on his shoulders; he would come into my tent at all hours of the night with his rolls of plans to flop down on my stretcher sighing how the pressure was really on. We would often go out together at first light in the morning to survey with extreme care and in some detail pegs for the teams to use when they arrived. One big job was the laying out of the anchorage bolts for the hundred foot high steel tower from which the bomb would be exploded. The holding-down bolts were to be in groups of four to each leg, each three feet long and set in six foot cubes of reinforced concrete, and the ultimate erection of the whole steel tower depended directly on the accuracy with which these were placed. The Whip and I planned it in my tent after midnight and we were out at dawn on the same morning which was Sunday. We laid it out on the ground with my theodolite, and he put in the thin nails in the wooden profiles. I had already precalculated the centre of this tower and marked it with a survey peg which at this stage looked the most unpretentious start to the scene of activity that was to follow. We had a bulldozed and graded road to it; alongside the road was the instrument lane with its toothpaste tubes, battleships, planes, and tanks.

"The Whip" and "Chinny" McWilliams

We checked and cross-checked the survey in such a way that it was exact to the thickness of the nails used. They were placed squarely about the little lone white painted centre peg. I had gone to no end of trouble to prove to myself that their positions were correct, for so much seemed to revolve about so little in every phase of this work that there was no room for errors or inaccuracy, and even the sceptics earlier on realized the importance of my initial trig survey of Area A.

It became normal to have either a bulldozer, grader, air-compressor, or concrete mixer breathing down my neck as I put in pegs in front of the theodolite. This flood of work was by no means confined to us; the maintenance workshops, too, were fighting to keep up. George Johnstone was the officer from the Mechanical Engineers in charge of this section and I overheard him one day, as he saw a mechanic with a spanner in one hand and a grease-gun in the other working on a vehicle, saying to the man in fun that he could at least have a screwdriver in his mouth as well. Barnie Bentley was his Sergeant-Major foreman who was possessed of almost supernatural powers as a "trouble-shooter" and could say what to look for in a sick engine by listening to it with his eyes closed. He was quiet and efficient, given to rare touches of subtle humour as was seen one time when he saw a man standing near him in the workshop. He suddenly turned and asked, "Don't you have anything to do?" At the affirmative reply, he asked incredulously as he pointed to the man's boots, "Then what are you doing standing there right alongside that patch of grease on the floor?" The mechanic trooped off forgetting all about the question he had meant to ask.

Few of the field parties had the time to place their vehicles in the hands of the workshops for maintenance for long at a time and as the smooth running of all parts of the work depended upon the continued service of the motor transport, a scheme was devised and put into practice. A mobile servicing lorry with every vehicle listed would go to each vehicle as its speedometer indicated and carry out repairs and service in the bush as its users worked. One day I returned to mine, theodolite over shoulder, to find it being attacked by mechanics replacing the radiator which they discovered had sprung a leak.

About this time Sir William Penney asked me to let him have a water-colour painting of an Australian Aborigine with a view to hanging it among typical souvenirs of his bomb trials in their official mess back in U.K. Each week as he asked how it was going I explained a start had been made, which really only meant that I had pinned the paper to my drawing board. There seemed so much to do that it was hard to fit this in, what with all the sums, but I couldn't disappoint him and did a little each night. One evening mealtime I had it finished and fetched it along to the mess rolled in a cardboard tube; it caught Sir William's attention instantly and he leapt up and grabbed it. Actually it was worth the trouble it had been to see how pleased he was as he opened it up.

A connecting road between two camera sites three or four miles apart became necessary, so we pegged it out and ran a bulldozer over it for its initial cut through the bush. We heard on the same day that in England the ceremony for the Coronation of the Queen had taken place, and named the road Coronation Parade to mark the event. On the way I came upon a small clearing with a depression in the centre which looked very like a native's former water supply and on closer inspection found definite evidence of its occupation by some nomad tribe from ages gone by. There was a pointed digging stick barely discernible, lying alongside the depression and some ancient black charcoal from fires. And this only five miles from where the first atomic bomb was to be tested in Australia! I couldn't help wondering what those long-dead tribes would have thought about it all. A new trig station which I sited on a stony ridge near by received the name of Yam Stick which appeared in all the subsequent calculations and on the top secret maps of the job.

The specially rigged out Rover vehicle I had been using throughout was finally showing signs of its beating and was passing the stage where normal maintenance could help it, so arrangements were made by radio with our H.Q. in Adelaide for securing a new one. On the return journey to Woomera I stayed at a friend's farm for the night and the farmer insisted that I house the sparkling new Land Rover in his shed out of the weather. I explained that it would be out for the rest of the year pushing through the bush with mulga branches raking at its sides and dust storms and heat battering at it but he removed his tractor to make room for it just the same.

One of the Padres from Woomera, Father Howell Witt, was due to make a visit to the camp about this time for the sorting out of any of the personal problems of the men, so we planned to make the trip out together in the new vehicle. On arrival at Woomera, however, I found something had cropped up which needed to be handled in a hurry so I left my new possession at the airport and flew out in a waiting York aircraft for the day, to put in another peg so a bulldozer wouldn't be held up. We were finally on our way. As we passed the various homesteads at the sheep stations the Padre wished to call in to help them and give impromptu services where required. At one such overnight stop there was a gathering to mark the engagement of one of the station daughters. Just as everything was going well, their lighting plant gave out plunging the homestead into darkness. Hurricane lamps and candles were lit and everyone trekked into the small building housing the engine, to offer what help and advice they could, and with the numbers present the room became packed to overflowing in such a way that nobody could move let alone attend to the trouble. At the height of the jostling the station mechanic yelled out above the noise something which I have never, to this day, been able to understand. "Would everyone please go out of the shed?" he shrieked, "because too many is worse than more than a lot."

The next day as we drove we heard the sound of an aeroplane engine close by and soon a light aircraft passed overhead so low that its wheels almost grazed the roof of my vehicle. Padre Witt reached out of the cabin window shaking his fist at the plane skimming along in front and called out "There goes my next door neighbour from Woomera and although I'll have something to say to him when I return, at least this is one time when he can't ask to borrow my lawn mower." As we passed the last station of Mabel Creek we stopped as usual by the open dam to see if there were any sheep bogged in the mud as they drank. Old Alf didn't worry with a fence or outside trough and many animals came to grief as a result. Sure enough there were half a dozen large sheep struggling in the mud so we went down the bank and started the job of extricating them foot by foot from the terrific suction and dragging them up the bank to safety. This meant getting into the mud with them, hob-nailed boots left on the dry ground. We strained and dragged at them for two hours until they were all free. Just as we topped the rise of the bank with the last one, a cloud of dust appeared on the horizon soon developing into an old station truck with several hands on board who had come to clean out the dam. As we drove slowly away with the drying mud falling off our still bare feet, the Padre sighed, "I don't mind looking after my lost sheep but heaven forgive me if I still wish those confounded hands had come along an hour earlier." He retained his clerical collar throughout and he did look a sight with rolled-up trousers over mud-caked blobs of feet, with the spotless white reversed collar on his khaki shirt.

That trip, long as it was, served as a welcome break, but as soon as Barnie's boys had given the new vehicle its checking out service we were straight back on the job. The tower anchorage blocks had set and the structure was progressing skywards by leaps and bounds, with huge angle iron girders lifted into place by means of a long wooden centre post used as a crane. I was secretly quite pleased that the pieces all seemed to fit together, although I knew the Whip and I couldn't have taken more care with the footings. The men using arc-welding machines were hanging about the steel structure like monkeys welding the gussets and plates into position as the trucks kept coming along with the component parts, and even the first stage of the tower seemed to me high off the ground as I climbed up. The ones on the construction of it became used to the gradually increasing distance from the ground as is usually the case and would walk along the girders without support of any kind. I noticed they maintained that casualness throughout its entire hundred feet of height.

While that was progressing an underground emplacement had to be opened up for the installation of a movie camera focused on a cathode ray tube which was planned to be triggered off seconds before the explosion to film the change in pattern of the green lines appearing on it. This was to be linked the mile and a half distance to more instruments at the bomb site; these instruments would disappear at the instant of firing but would record valuable information up to that time. The co-axial cable link was to be buried under five feet of overburden, and as the intermediate terrain was still solid travertine a surface scratch was made with a bulldozer and ripper, and the covering was heaped over it laboriously ten feet at a time throughout the distance with another dozer. The blasting of the great hole in this travertine was a highlight even for the ever bubbling-over Chinny McWilliams, keen for constant noise and action. Dozens of deep holes were bored with jack hammers into the rock, each of which was rammed full with plugs of gelignite and joined to a main lone detonator by instantaneous fuse. This work went on for days until the spot was loaded with cases of high explosives plug by plug under the ground. McWilliams was in his element and as excited as a boy on Guy Fawkes' night in anticipation of the violence of the imminent blasting.

Soon the day arrived, and the short length of safety fuse was ignited. We already had my Land Rover engine running and pointing in a direction away from the scene but now with the sight of the spluttering fuse so fresh in our memory Chinny and

I drove it well away like fury and turned to see the show. In less than a minute there was the most enormous upheaval this quiet bush country had ever known and great slabs of rock shot into the sky to rain down at intervals of time, varying according to their bulk. When it had subsided we drove back to the gaping hole to check whether it had been completely successful, and a bulldozer had soon lumbered on to the area to clean up. McWilliams used the rest of the explosive to clear away a huge stump, but in this case there must have been some miscalculation, for we returned to the new Land Rover to find it firmly wedged into the passenger's seat hurled there through the open door. It took us an hour to chop and lever it out to enable Chinny to return with me to camp.

As the tower was nearing completion a set of guide rails was scheduled to be welded into place to take the cradle which would transport the atomic bomb itself to the top, and a set of small railway lines emerging from a locked shed alongside to a point under the guides would be the means of rolling the weapon into place. Periodically I would visit the tower to line the guide rails into position using the theodolite crosswires, while the Whip climbed about the structure marking the spots. During one of these trips when the small railway bedding was to be installed, I transferred the position of my old survey peg to the concrete, and these engineers, used to handling tons of concrete, thought the big pouring job of a spoonful of their cement around my brass plug was a huge joke.

I could not know what a shock was in store for me when I set out one morning from the bomb site to the village along the helicopter road. Usually I stayed out until dark every day but this morning some extra sums were needed, so I had to return to my "office." Driving along in the bright, clear morning, I happened to observe a large tip-truck coming towards me for another load of rubble. In such an encounter the bigger trucks had precedence over the smaller. Just as I was preparing to make the detour, the large lorry suddenly swerved off the road to come to rest against a mound of bulldozed dirt alongside. I wondered at this, knowing that it was up to me to avoid him, and slowed down to see if he could get the truck free from the mound. To my astonishment I noticed him seemingly sound asleep lying over his wheel, so I called out to him. There was no answer. Growing a little alarmed I switched off and walked over, climbed up on his running board, and shook him, causing his head to roll off the steering wheel and slump on his shoulder. More alarmed than ever I got down and opened his door. His arm flopped by his side and hung lifelessly. This looked serious so I pulled him out of his seat, laid him across my shoulders and carried him to my vehicle where I put him along the front seats. There was no breath vapour from a rear vision mirror placed at his open mouth, and there was no sign of a pulse in his wrist. I had heard of people occasionally dropping dead at the controls of their vehicles but I was very shaken to realize that I had apparently just witnessed such an occurrence with my own eyes.

I noticed a York warming up on the Claypan for take-off so bunching up his knees, slamming the door, and cradling his head on my lap as I drove, I raced for a field telephone to contact the control tower to tell them to hold the plane for an emergency. I saw the propellers soon come to a stop, and then rushed him up to the camp to arrange his evacuation. A friend of his gathered some of his personal belongings and climbed aboard to accompany "the body" to Woomera. Word spread like wild fire, and a profound gloom settled immediately over the camp.

We heard later that while they were on the plane the "dead man" had suddenly sat up and sleepily asked where he was. His tent mate sitting alongside who had resigned himself to the fact that he had died at the wheel of his tip-truck had apparently all but passed out himself at the "corpse's" unexpected action. White-faced and trembling he endeavoured to explain what had happened—they were aboard a York aircraft high over the mulga on their way to check up with the Woomera doctors.

Their report showed that he had had a temporary heart failure that had sent him into a complete coma and that after observation he would be allowed to return. The coincidence was that he was scheduled to take part in a radio programme by singing a song— he was something of an expert in that line—due to take place in less than a fortnight's time. In the meantime I had to make a quick flight to Adelaide for two days. The night I was there I visited some friends who told me of the expected broadcast from Woomera and turned on their radio for us all to hear. Sure enough the "body" was introduced and put on his act at the end of which I informed my friends that not two weeks ago I had dragged his apparently dead body from a truck in Central Australia. It sounded too incredible to be true, even to me.

When we landed at Woomera the next day on the return trip to the Claypan the same man approached to thank me for what he had been told I had done for him, and all I could say as I saw him "alive" again was that he had indeed given me rather a surprise.

Dingoes were proving troublesome to the cable-layers at Emu. Men were constantly discovering lines severed by the dogs' sharp teeth. It soon became a problem of sizeable proportions which had to be solved, so the electronic experts in Maddock's section got on the job and produced the most unique method of coping with it ever seen in the Outback. First, they obtained a dead dingo and carefully measured the distance from the front paws to its mouth. To this they added a safety margin of twice the length of its tongue plus the distance measured on the ground of the shoulders forward of the paws which it would be possible for it to reach without losing its centre of gravity, and doubled the final result. This gave them the dimensions of a plate of steel cut into a square which they had made in the welders' shop; they then wired several strategically placed units to a circuit calculated to kill instantly without pain. A rheostat controlled the amperage and a meaty bait was placed in the punched centre of the square. This meant that a dingo approaching from any direction would necessarily be forced to step on the plate with its forepaws in order to be able to reach the meat. A moat of tomato juice surrounded the plate for an effective slow-drying earth connection and in the first night there were seven cable breakers fewer, and soon the rest of the wiring was safe at last. Although the old bush professional government doggers had many tricks up their sleeves to catch their quarry, I'm sure this would have been something new to them.

There seemed to be no end to the boxes and crates comprising Maddock's stuff and they continued to arrive on the Yorks. The half-round huts being erected to house it all, had their longest axes pointed towards the bomb tower four miles away. Both end walls were capable of removal to allow the bomb blast to carry right on unmolested by anything. Every building at the forward area was of similar construction and it looked like being quite an event when the trial eventually took place.

Frank Hill's collection of plants and specimens pickled in their jars of formalin was growing daily and he began to send them in crates back to England for further study. One day I saw him rush out of his tent with a sheaf of papers, fling them into the air, and retreat as they rained down into the saltbush by the hundred. Several hours later I noticed him going around carefully picking them all up again and taking them inside once more. My curiosity aroused and knowing full well that the very last thing he could ever be subject to was a violent temper, I asked him about it. It seems they were papers which were placed either side of botanical specimens prior to pressing and to prevent fungus developing from the slight moisture in the plants, they were periodically taken from the press and dried out in the sun. This was the simplest way to disperse them for the process. Jars of all sizes, sealed and containing more varied specimens than

I had ever seen in the bush, were sent back on the special planes bound regularly for the U.K. After the project was over Frank received special recognition there for his conscientious work and effort.

With all the mountains of work to be got through, I remember how it was brought home to me how little time we had left to look after ourselves. A friend mentioned to me quite innocently that he had to attend a fancy dress ball dressed as a ragged old dead-beat, and enquired if he could possibly borrow my clothes for the best effect. I believe he won the prize.

10

The Concert

So many men both at the bomb site itself, and at the headquarters at Woomera and at Salisbury had done so much constant work with such willingness, many far beyond what was required of them officially, that ideas for a short relaxation of the tension began to take shape. A "concert committee" was formed with the full sanction of everyone involved. It was to plan a never-to-be-forgotten event in the life at the Claypan and invitations were to be extended to all who had a hand in the smooth running of the programme from their desks at H.Q.

The idea caught on with immediate success and Luke helped with whatever was needed for the occasion. The actors and performers would come from the camp, volunteering whatever talents hidden or otherwise they possessed. Soon an impressive list of artists was drawn up: Lorry Hogan, an airfield construction foreman could play the bagpipes which Chinny McWilliams promised to obtain, Ken Hurne, the cook mostly to be seen peeling onions in the kitchen was a hypnotist, the once "dead" tip-truck driver could sing, and an orderly room sergeant was an expert on the piano. Of course, the fact that there wasn't a piano for many hundreds of miles didn't present any problem, as Luke was to confiscate one from a source he knew about and have it flown out to the Claypan specially for the event. A heavy equipment fitter, strangely enough, could tune a piano but couldn't play a note. I added what I could to the programme by volunteering to draw with wax lumber crayon on huge sheets of butcher's paper, caricatures of various well-known members of the camp. Throughout the project so far, John Stanier had been taking reels of colour movie films of the boys as they worked, so he was to fetch them along with the equipment to give a local film show on the night.

All the preparation for the concert, planned for several weeks hence on a Saturday night, was done by the ones concerned, with ample help from the others by lamplight after their normal day's work. The first essential was a stage. Carpenters set about building this with whatever materials they could find. The platform was comprised of a number of tent floor boards. A white picket fence screened off the future "orchestra pit" and the whole thing was built at the foot of the hill where the village had sprung up. It was complete with side-walls and a roof with a butcher's paper lining on which I drew the stage props. Maddock and his team supplied a microphone and stand wired to loud speakers tied to the mulga trees. These were probably the most easily obtained pieces of equipment present.

Looking at the finished product I was reminded of an incident which had occurred before in a bush town where the people suddenly required a similar sort of stage for a visiting entertainment group. A man returning to his house one afternoon was astounded to see only a vacant block of land where the house used to be, so he hurried to the small police station to report that he had a complaint to make. When the constable asked what it was, he replied, "Some coot went an' pinched me 'ouse." No one could find the house anywhere, but as the man was sitting watching the performance that evening he recognized parts of the stage as being from his front veranda. On closer inspection he discovered the whole structure had been built with the component parts of his bachelor dwelling.

As soon as the set of bagpipes arrived, Lorry started rehearsals and kept them up for so long at a time that various members seemed to think they would like a spell from listening. Eventually one of the chemists poured a test-tube full of some mysterious liquid down one of the drones. This proceeded to eat great holes

The Centurion tank came part of the way by loader
. . . and was driven the rest

in the bag itself until it was nothing more than a network of openings held together with strips of hide. Lorry was very disappointed and brought what had once been his bagpipes to me to see what could be done.

I happened to have a well-tanned kangaroo skin in my box so offered to try to make a new bag for the instrument. Carefully taking what was left of the old one and unpicking the stitches I laid it out on the 'roo skin and cut out the pearshaped piece to fit. The bullet-hole in the skin could be manoeuvred until it coincided with one of the holes cut to take a drone, so it would be completely airtight. With waxed string and huge sail needle from the cable joiners' kit, I sewed it together and tightly tied each drone, the mouthpiece, and the hand reed tube into place. Dressed it with its tartan sack covering it looked quite as good as new, although I had never seen a set of pipes before. Only then did I tentatively try to blow it up. Alas, all the air I could muster seeped out of the needle holes as fast as I blew it in, and each time my only reward was a feeble sound like a duck dying. I called Hogan in but he was quite unperturbed. He said that this often happened and was easily taken care of by the insertion of a weak mixture of treacle and hot water to heal over the holes. Sure enough this worked like a charm and, much to the sorrow of the chemist, Hogan was soon practising again. The only thing wrong was that as the sweet goo oozed out on to the tartan jacket, the whole thing was constantly set upon by ants and flies, forcing him to carry a tin of repellent in his camp-made sporran. He nevertheless refused to let it out of his sight from then on, sleeping and working with it literally under his arm all the time.

Next came the Scottish dress and kilt to go with it for his big stage act. The tartan for the kilt, cap, and plaid was made by spraying a red-lead soaked scrubbing brush over a piece of yellow survey bunting cloth which was placed under a piece of steel concrete reinforcing arc mesh. This gave a square red pattern and the lines in between the squares were hand-painted with a

The bomb tower
Rails for the atomic bomb trolley
Toothpaste tube baffle plates

toothbrush dipped in a huge mulga green paint pot. The black belt across the chest and around his waist was made from the tarred malthoid that is sometimes used for fowl house roofs, cut into wide strips and dipped in petrol to make them a shiny black. His sporran was composed of a row of frayed-out manilla rope trimmed to length with an axe, emerging from beneath a half section of an aluminium saucepan lid, engraved with the end of a wood rasp. Tucked in his spats made of army gaiters dipped in whitewash, was the traditional dirk which was really a cook's carving knife. He was to wear some pink lace underpants rescued from the sack of bulldozer engineers' cleaning rags. From a relatively short distance the whole effect was as perfect as we non-Scotsmen could wish to see.

One day the piano appeared among the loading on a York. Many helping hands got it aboard a waiting lorry, rolling it along on lengths of bore casing and unloading it in the "orchestra pit" by the stage. The sergeant musician soon found it to be well out of tune so the bulldozer mechanic spent a good proportion of time fixing it up. Finally, he declared it to be in tune and the sergeant was overjoyed to find that it really was. A large canvas camp sheet tied down over it kept off the sun until the night. A long length of fencing wire was stretched diagonally over where the audience was to sit in a natural ampitheatre on the slope of the hill, and a large steel outline of the project's code number "X200" was made by the welders, and was joined and attached to the wire by rollers. This was bound in yards of potato bagging wired into place, the idea being that at the opening this would be soaked in petrol, ignited, and released to roll slowly in flames on the wire over the patrons. Most of this was for the benefit of the unsuspecting visitors from H.Q. of course, as we wanted them to have some stories of the Claypan hospitality to take back with them.

Tents and stretchers were prepared to accommodate them overnight. Chinny and I tied two bundles of gelignite to two myall trees just safely over the rim of a small vertical cliff at the end of the tent lines. These were to have detonators and different lengths of safety fuses attached which would be lit by us simultaneously at five o'clock on the morning following the concert. The theory here was that when one fuse gave out and set off its bundle of explosive, the visitors, still half asleep, would probably land on the floor of their tents from the shock; then, as they struggled back into their blankets in a daze, they would be allowed a minute to settle in before the next fuse came to its end, thus initiating the next and more violent explosion. We visualized the unfortunate H.Q. men sitting trembling on the edge of their beds nervously awaiting the next one but there were to be no more. All the Claypan members had been forewarned, as we had to live together for a long time to come. Sir William Penney was tickled pink at the ingenuity of the diabolical scheme.

Three whole cases of gelignite placed in an oil drum were set at a distance worked out by Chinny who was in charge of the explosion. To start the show off with a bang they were all to be ignited at the same time at a signal given by the petrol-soaked blazing inferno of the "X200" sign glowing up into the sky. The lighting and rolling of the sign were to be initiated after twenty coloured phosphorous Verey pistol flares were fired in a criss-cross pattern over the "theatre-goers'" heads, and to make sure the men ready to release the sign did not lose count, the last two shots were to be of a different colour. Only accurate timing would produce the best effect, and the differently coloured flares would also be the signal for the exact length of safety fuse at the oil drum to be lit to give McWilliams time to drive away in a hurry before it exploded.

I was beginning to think the preparation for the concert was giving us more work if possible than the preparation for the atomic bomb itself, but it kept the morale at its usual high level.

Once a date was set for the night everyone started secretly rehearsing plays and acts in earnest. Ken Hurne tried out the best subjects for his hypnotic act and demonstrated his powers to us from time to time, soon proving he was quite expert in the art. Apparently he had worked with a well-known performer before he joined the Army as a cook.

The amount of talent to be found in a camp of this nature was amazing—it looked as if we would be able to put on a good bush show. I selected a dozen of the boys from all spheres to cartoon on the stage from "memory" but really I had already made a number of sketches beforehand for the best effect. Among the subjects I chose were the Whip, Luke, McWilliams, Flip, and one of the tall thin plumbers with the baggiest overalls I had ever seen.

The three Yorks made available to fly the visitors in began arriving on the morning of the concert. Everything had been planned—as well as the short nerve-racking journey from the aeroplanes to the village. Being organized by McWilliams it consisted mostly of gelignite and revolver shots. The security section looking as stern and official as they could met each visitor as he emerged from the plane and inspected his pass. This was routine but they really did not have to wear shiny leather shoulder holsters holding huge .45 automatics. The office workers stared wide-eyed at them and moved obediently into their allotted trucks to proceed in convoy to the village.

Mountain Lowrey led the convoy in a utility buckboard at a pre-calculated speed of five miles per hour, arriving opposite a thick clump of myalls at the exact time a bundle of buried explosive was set to go off. The signal to light the fuse was given by a security officer who fired three quick shots from his automatic as Mountain left for the village. Just the right-sized shock wave blasted the sides of the trucks and anyone wearing a hat suddenly found himself bareheaded. This was to condition them for the evening's events.

They were shown their tents and as they beat at the clouds of flies and gratefully sat down for a rest after the long flight, they were completely unaware of what was to come. When it came to retaining secret information the Emu boys were tops. After a wonderful meal put on specially by Ozzie and his boys, it was time for them to take their places at the amphitheatre, and by five minutes to eight everything was ready for the performance.

At three minutes to eight the bucket of petrol was sprayed over the sign and the hessian was well soaked, as, to the obvious surprise of the audience, the phosphorous flare signals began coming from all directions. With the second one of a different colour a lighted match was thrown at the sacking around the sign which burst into flames shooting up into the night and the thin retaining wire was cut by a mechanic with a pair of pliers. The roaring "X200" slowly passed over the heads of the terrified visitors and at the precise moment it plunged into the lower myall tree, the oil drum containing the three cases of gelignite on a rise half a mile away exploded in a sheet of white hot flame. Seconds later the roar of the shock wave carrying the violence of the blast, hit the group sitting in surely one of the most unusual theatres ever. By this time most of them were as white as the scene on the ridge, but then the floodlights were switched on bathing the stage in a glare of the same old shade of white and the sergeant opened the proceedings with a burst on the piano which had been uncovered in the darkness. The "live" corpse came on stage to the microphone with a very professionally rendered song to the accompaniment of the piano, and the show was under way.

One of the members of the stone-picking group of engineers, a short round and jolly corporal, was M.C. He had compered many army gatherings in the past and did an excellent job keeping the periods in between acts bubbling with jokes. I felt sure the colour was returning to the faces of the visitors at last.

The Cinderella opera was next on the programme. Although this particular version would hardly be suitable for the drawing-room, it was cleverly done; a lot of work had been put into it. The hobnailed boot "glass slipper" which was attached to a myall branch overhanging the stage, almost hit Cinderella on the head, but glanced off her shoulder as it fell.

After another piano item Ken Hurne called for complete silence which the visitors were more than willing to give. He mass hypnotized his six subjects and put them through a variety of harmless acts. One was so successfully hypnotized that he was laid with his shoulders on one chair and his feet on another, and a man standing on his belt line didn't even bend him. The whole act was a most interesting addition to the show and all onlookers were suitably amazed at seeing such sights in so remote a setting.

My caricatures came next amid much yelling and comments as the various ones were recognized. I think the Whip drew the most vigorous reception and after I had finished up with Brigadier Luke everyone called out that I would be out of a job the next day. Actually he asked for a smaller one to keep for himself later. I was forced to hurry with each one because the soft wax lumber crayon tended to melt in my hand with the heat of the lights.

Lorry Hogan carried on the show with a very well put over bagpipe solo. He looked no different from the lone piper who appears at the Edinburgh Festival—that is to anyone who hadn't been there. Old Jock who had won the old codgers' race might have thought otherwise but it was still an excellent performance. He finished his act in the middle of his rendition of "Nut Brown Maiden" by suddenly stopping and gasping loudly as he trudged off the stage for all to hear, "That's all fellers, I've had it."

While the movie projector was being prepared, the pianist and the M.C. kept things going. Then, with the white tent fly unrolled for a screen, the colour movie started rolling, with all the "film stars" sitting right in the audience watching themselves and each other. A roar went up as, one by one, the boys appeared on the screen, and friends yelled appropriate remarks about each character. There were some action shots of the army engineers at the bottoms of excavations shovelling out rubble and if the

one on the shovel happened to stop to lean on the handle for a
spell, the audience would bawl a phrase they had heard the Whip
use, such as "Get working down there, this isn't a convalescent
camp; move about now." Although Ken Garden had his sense of
humour, he was seldom to be seen other than serious-faced with
the numerous things on his mind, and when he appeared on the
canvas smiling, a particularly rugged air force member of the
airfield construction team yelled out at the top of his voice,

Larry Hogan carried on the show with a bagpipe solo.

"There y'are, what did I tell you blokes, it *can* laugh if it wants to."
It was all taken in good part by everyone and this was a highly
successful finish to the most lively and appreciated concert that
could be found anywhere in Australia.

The visitors were delighted to have been invited to it and would
return to their desks at H.Q. with a renewed interest and under-

standing of what was involved. Until now they had thought of the project only in terms of impersonal code numbers and reams of paper work.

Finally they trudged wearily to their tents. They were unused to this sort of activity and they had already made a long flight that day and would be leaving the next morning at first light. Soon they were lying on their beds, exhausted and rapidly drifting into welcome oblivion. But Lorry Hogan was not going to let them off so lightly—he walked slowly up and down their tent lines vigorously playing "Nut Brown Maiden" on his kangaroo skin bagpipes. The ants would have to wait for their treacle and water supply; even we thought it might be nice when it stopped. Eventually it did—at three in the morning.

At half-past four McWilliams crept into my tent and we prepared to go down to light the fuses on the bundles of gelignite hidden by the small cliff at the end of the camp lines. They were to go off at five a.m., so, at that time, with match heads placed firmly on the ends of the angle-cut fuses, Chinny and I drew the edge of the matchbox across them simultaneously and raced for our respective tents. A minute later a violent explosion rang out. This was followed by a shock wave making the tents shudder in spite of the slight subduing caused by the cliff. Things were quiet for the succeeding minute during which time we could only speculate on the reactions of our friends. With watch held tightly in hand, I counted down to the second and bigger explosion. Within seconds of the allotted minute which seemed an hour even to us, the next bundle went off and this all but blew the nearer tents down. Now those who had been warned could resume their interrupted sleep. Not so the visitors who could be heard gasping and asking each other what on earth had happened. As we had expected, they waited in vain for the third.

Soon, however, the whole camp was astir and willing hands began moving the heavy piano from the orchestra pit to the aeroplane. It was loaded and securely tied down to the holding bolts in the York. By this time Ozzie, Ken, and the kitchen staff had an excellent breakfast prepared for everyone.

The visitors were then shown some of the "sights" of the Claypan. They saw the fly-covered rubbish dump, and the "Tiefa" machine that was used daily to force clouds of white fumes into the middle of swarms of insects in the quarry and at the water bore sites. A visit to the forward area was not included in the itinerary but an inspection of our prized new concrete mixer filled in the time until the accompanying aircraft fitters had their planes serviced, refuelled, and ready for the return journey to Woomera and Adelaide. We couldn't quite fathom the reason for the gleam in the eyes of the pilots as we drove the thoroughly weary but still smiling passengers down to the Claypan. They gratefully handed in their temporary passes, had their names checked off the lists by the security section who kept up the atmosphere to the last with their grim faces and their .45s in shoulder holsters, and disappeared with a wary backward glance over their shoulders to sink into their seats.

The whole thing had certainly gone off with a bang, and stories of the rugged Claypan camp were to be heard at H.Q. for weeks to come. But the most important thing was that they all had actually survived and were really glad they had come. The engines of the three planes started as soon as the doors had been slammed shut, a little too soon, we thought, but the haste went almost unnoticed. They taxied to the extremity of the Claypan, turned, warmed up their motors, and commenced their take-off runs one after the other. We could almost hear the sighs of our friends as they waved from the windows.

However, the master touch was yet to come. The three huge aircraft circled and seemingly got themselves manoeuvred into one straight line, nose to tail as would a ground convoy, and made what we thought was a final pass over the Claypan, as we watched from the ground. Then, without warning, they made a graceful sweep a mile or so on the Woomera side of the camp, and flying lower and lower as they approached the lines of tents, screamed at tree top level over our canvas bedrooms. The first one loosened most of them in the slipstream, the second demolished those and handled others, and the third, exactly in the same line as the others with propellers almost touching the tail rudder of the one in front completely flattened most of the remaining tents, keeping up and increasing the violent suction of the others' slipstream. As the three monsters rose from the trees with a well-timed banking operation they put their noses down once more and really excelled themselves at low formation flying as they all made another obviously pre-planned pass over our humble, flattened abodes, dealing with several on the outskirts which had so far survived.

When we reached the scene of utter destruction we could almost hear those pilots and passengers saying, "That'll teach you," as they rapidly became three black specks in the sky on their way south. It had been our turn to be on the receiving end and, as we sat among the wreckage, we laughed until tears came to our eyes. It had surely solved the riddle of the gleam in the pilots' eyes and the eagerness with which they had started their engines as the doors slammed.

So ended what was undoubtedly the most raucous week-end that could have been endured anywhere on our planet, and one that could not have happened anywhere else but in the remote outback setting of the Central Australian bush. Everyone on both sides had been "entertained" to the limit and a more fitting and well-earned lull in the pressure on all those present, could not have been possible.

As we began the job of rebuilding our village, I overheard one of the weary boys remark, "When Hogan's bagpipes break down again, we'll sure make him a new bag, but this time it will be out of Beadell's skin."

11

Into It Once More

The concert had been a brief interlude, but now it had to be forgotten. As soon as the flattened sleeping quarters were restored, we attacked operations once more with renewed vigour. The Whip appeared at my tent with his inevitable roll of plans and we began again with the planning of the operation ahead.

The tower was nearing completion and had become part of the landscape, soaring as it did out of the unbroken scrub-covered undulations of Area A. I had marked the vertical row of pencil lines on both sides of the square structure opposite to its peak, where the final lengths of guide rails were to be welded. A steel stairway resembling a fire escape was already built almost to the top. "Shorty," one of the expert arc welders who had been hanging from the girders throughout its construction, invited me to try my hand at it one day as he had neared the ninety foot mark by then. The electric cables to the generator which became longer and heavier as he went up had to be attached to the nearest cross-stay by heavy straps. I climbed the ladder and cautiously edged along a transom to where he was working. The other terminal had been clipped to a huge steel gusset which had to be welded to both members of a junction and I was thankful that I didn't have to hang by my knees to reach it as I had seen him do so many times before. Of course in that attitude he had appeared the right way up through the normally inverting optical lenses of my theodolite as I saw him from the ground. I had seen a human face wearing goggles, and with the action of gravity all his face muscles were on the top of his countenance, and his long hair seemed to stand straight up from his scalp.

Now, however, I was in his place clinging on to the handpiece with one hand, and the electric welding rod with the other. At least I was the right way up. I tried to "hit 'er with the arc" as they say but succeeded only in anchoring the rod solidly to the structure. With a few words of professional advice from Shorty, I tried again and got the molten metal running along the join forming what I had been told was a fillet weld. The only way this appeared to be possible, apart from getting it arcing in the first place, was to keep the rod from actually touching the job. I felt quite pleased with my efforts as I crawled back to the relative safety of the stairway, but any personal satisfaction I felt was quickly dispelled as I heard an independent foreman welder who saw the job say to Shorty, "Who done it, the cook?"

The bomb tower was such a massive structure that I wondered what would happen to it on *the* day. The Englishmen asked me how I thought it would stand up to the blast and I replied that the top section would probably be blown right off, and the upper half would quite likely be very much strained; possibly only the lower fifty feet would remain unhurt. They merely grinned broadly and said "You'll see."

One morning an extremely unpleasant accident was narrowly averted at the tower. There was some woodwork needed on top to nail some wiring on to, and in order to help, Mountain Lowrey and I climbed the hundred feet with a hand rip-saw to cut off some surplus beams. The piece to be severed was tied securely to a near-by steel strut with a length of rope to prevent it falling, and Mountain began the job with the saw. In no time the job was completed and the piece fell off to swing freely a foot lower. But the heat of the day and the effort had made his hand slippery with sweat, and the saw suddenly fell from his grasp and dropped end over end towards the ground between the legs of the tower. We both looked down and were horrified to see a man working within the bounds of the footings. We did not dare shout a warning in case he moved in the wrong direction.

The saw was hurtling straight at him one instant and veering about as the air caught the flat faces of the blade the next. We held our breath for the next few seconds, when suddenly a gust of wind moved its vertical downward path to one side of the guide rails and it crashed on to the concrete not two feet from the still unsuspecting man. He involuntarily threw up his hands and looked up at us in the second before the shock set in as he realized how close he had been to almost certain death. Then he threw down the engineers' hammer that he had been using and rushed for the bomb-arming shed which stood alongside at the end of the small railway track. Allan Lowrey and I looked at each other— too shaken to speak. We were trembling as we climbed silently down the flights of steel rungs.

Fortunately, there was a lighter side to our work. One day as I drove along with the Whip to where he had a team opening out another underground emplacement he leapt out of the vehicle and lumbered to the edge of the hole. He brusquely told the man on the shovel to climb out of the hole. The man readily complied, but was told by old Ernie May to get back in again. He had no sooner reached the bottom than he was ordered to return immediately to the surface. When the bewildered man asked what was going on he was told by the wily Whip to "Keep going . . . You're bringing more dirt out on your boots each time than you were with the shovel." Even the tired man burst out laughing.

Another time I noticed a heavily laden tip-truck well bogged down in the sand. The driver, reluctant to dump his load to help himself get out, had churned the wheels until the axle housings were resting firmly on the surface. A bulldozer driver working in a near-by quarry brought his huge machine over to the rescue, and they attached his logging winch cable firmly to the front steel bumper bar of the stricken lorry. I watched as the drivers climbed aboard and the bulldozer operator pulled in the master clutch lever. It wasn't until the husky plant operator was well ahead and steering to the safety of the harder ground that he glanced around to see only the bumper bar of the tipper following. The truck had not moved. The bumper bar had been gently torn clean off the ends of the massive chassis, shearing the holding rivets and bolts neatly level as though they had been made of butter. The truck driver didn't even stir from his seat at the wheel; he only drummed his fingers slowly on the gear lever, and, with his hat pushed back on his head, laconically made his assessment of the situation. "They just don't make them like they used to."

Weary Willie of the "finish up I finished up" fame would often not bother with proper pronunciation, and when a newly arrived and nervous scientist happened to ask him what they would do in the event of an aircraft fire on the Claypan, Willie, always ready to help if he could, assured him that everything was under control. "They keep one of them big fire distinguishers at one end specially for that."

Apparently an atomic bomb needs a smaller pilot bomb to start it off, probably in the same way in which a detonator is needed to explode a plug of gelignite. These smaller bombs, known as "Kittens," have to be tested, and it now was time to hold a series of "Kittens trials." As the bombs were very small, although still radiation producing, trials could be held closer in without any risk whatsoever, so, less than six miles from the village, I pegged out three miles of new road along which these trials were to take place.

It was not long after that that we drove along to witness the "inaugural bang" at Emu. Never having seen a nuclear explosion of any kind, I was inclined to wish I were somewhere else. Had it not been for the experts comprising the Kittens team standing alongside during the countdown I would have been. At the word "now" there was quite a dainty explosion that twisted a steel framework around as if it had been caught up in a whirlwind; the team were very satisfied. At the completion of their vital part in the main event they lost no time in returning to their families in England; their work had been successfully accomplished. The

Kittens' turn-off junction was to assume value out of all imaginable proportions in several weeks' time, in a most unexpected way . . . and it had nothing whatsoever to do with the Emu project.

Some of the carpenters got together, and, with suggestions from a visiting line construction expert, Aub Reilly from Woomera, designed and fashioned a mulga wood medal that was to be presented to Sir William Penney at a special ceremony. It consisted of a section of a mulga tree trunk four inches in diameter, turned on the wood lathe to resemble a wooden pulley wheel, into whose groove was nestled a coiled spiral of copper wire. This had been polished with emery and clear lacquered to preserve its sheen, while the wooden disc had had oils and varnishes applied to prevent it cracking, and was polished to a glass finish. There was an inscription on one side engraved in gold, and a huge fencing wire clip attached to the back for pinning to his pocket—assuming the pocket was strong enough to hold it. All things considered the completed "medal" was an excellent job.

At the ceremony Sir William was required to come forward for the presentation; a citation about his being the jolliest nuclear scientist of the year was read, and the medal was duly hung on his pocket. But with the constant washing in hard bore water, the stitches of the garment had weakened, and the whole pocket almost tore off under the weight. Sir William was delighted and gave the expected response. Then he replaced the decoration in its mulga wood box with its cotton wool lining (from the first aid post) before he lost his pocket completely. Later, when I visited England, I saw how much he treasured our gift—the medal from Emu was hanging in pride of place above his study desk in his home.

One day a small ominous looking box measuring about a foot cube arrived on a Hastings aircraft from England. It was placed on a truck to be taken to a sealed-off shed. One of the English team, Schilling, casually asked me if I would pass it to him, so, eager to help, I grasped the carrying handle. It was like trying to lift up the truck as well so I tried with both hands; still I could not move it and I was beginning to think it must be bolted down to the lorry. I saw the joke he had played as he was laughing out loud by now. Apparently the only thing capable of making an impression on it was the mobile crane. The box was lined with solid lead leaving a small cavity to house some weird radioactive material at its core; the lid was of similar construction. Schilling, who had a little joke about himself being "twelve better than Penney," continued to have his fun with anyone who was unsuspecting.

In due course the bomb-casing itself arrived under canvas coverings on a huge semi-trailer driven by my old friend, Bill Lloyd. Cradled in semi-circular wooden chairs, it was hurried to the screened-off processing sheds and was not seen again by most of us except for the morning it was put on the firing tower to show us what it could do. A special security guard was set up to live alongside the shed containing the other end of the small railway, and the cipher communications soon became more taboo than ever. With the arrival of certain important items and with the strengthening of security at the camp, we at last felt that the end of the job was in sight.

When Luke was approached by some despairing technician or mechanic and asked to obtain a vital part or piece of equipment, he took up the challenge immediately and was always ready to fight for what he wanted. One day he contacted by radio an H.Q. man concerning a mechanical part for an important motor. He was advised that the part was not available. But Luke was not to be daunted. "Who's your boss . . . Well, who's *his* boss . . . Then put me on to him," he said. On being told positively that it was not available in Australia, Luke sent a top priority signal to the makers of the motor in Detroit and within a week the "unobtainable" part was right at our Claypan direct from the U.S.A. He didn't forget to quote some appropriate biblical phrase to those "defeatists" either. He was so pleased with what he considered one of his greatest victories that he came to me rubbing his hands, and asked me to draw a political cartoon that could be reproduced and distributed to all concerned including the Ministers of the Government Departments involved in the Federal Capital at Canberra.

We devised an "X200 tiger" with the code worked into its stripes, wearing spurs and standing over a desk worker in his office who was meekly surrendering with a white handkerchief tied to a fountain pen. A copy was given to Howard Beale the current Minister for Supply in Australia and one handed to Mr Duncan Sandys from the U.K. when he visited the Claypan. It was a great success and didn't fail to bring the results Luke was looking for.

There was never a dull moment. One night we photographed the total eclipse of the moon that had been predicted by the observatories. With our cameras set up on tripods and everyone watching as the time drew near, we saw what appeared to be a piece cut out of the full moon. As it increased in size we took photographs of it on the same negative, adjusting the exposure as the light diminished. Our processed films gave an interesting one-picture record of the event.

I even found time to draw several murals on the white caneite lining of the mess room. On the end wall panels I did a huge portrait of what I thought was a typical Englishman wearing pince-nez glasses and wing collar. He was looking through a window at the typical Australian bush, while a wild myall Aborigine looked right back, laughing at all the frenzied effort going on inside. Another showed Frank Hill catching a miniature flying helicopter in a specimen net. Later the whole panels were sawn clear, crated between table tennis boards, and, under the name of special plans were shipped to England for the H.Q. there. The Englishmen would stop at nothing to preserve something they valued. When a brochure was published for prospective employees at the Atomic Weapons Research Establishment there, I was sent a copy, and I noticed a glossy reproduction of the portraits.

One morning about this time Alan Woolley complained of a slight sickness and discomfort and was absent from several meals. The pains grew until he could stand them no longer, and he was carefully placed, white-faced, on a plane for Woomera. Upon arrival the doctors immediately took out his appendix which, they said, would have burst had he delayed another day. In an amazingly short time he was back with us, still white-faced and nursing his wound continually until he had fully recovered, but at least he *was* back with us.

In the ante-room attached to the mess there was a steadily growing assortment of newspaper and magazine cartoons pertaining to our project coming from all over the world. Front pages were devoted to the stories as they emerged from the Claypan and an official press party was finally permitted to visit our Claypan and write up whatever they saw. There were regular comic strip characters using this as a subject for their current series of jokes and articles of all sizes from periodicals. The best ones were cut out and pinned to the walls. It served at least to show that we had come a long way from the morning of the Eyebrows conference with Bill Worth, and even from the four-poster outdoor bed at the northern fringe and entrance to Area A. The first atomic bomb to be tested on our mainland of Australia was receiving even more than its expected nation-wide interest.

Several camera towers whose bases incorporated Nissen huts with dark rooms for handling film had been completed. They were designed to give a three-way intersecting cut of the explosion by the dozens of cameras installed in each. At the pressing of the single button at the firing control desk each camera would be set off automatically. Many miles of cable were involved in the process; some had to be buried under access roads and others, as in the case of Coronation Parade to the Camera C tower, could be simply unrolled alongside the bulldozed road. We had to lay out the footings for the camera towers carefully, so that they would be facing the bomb tower which at that stage was not visible.

Posts were dotted about at required intervals with steel cylinders directed at the tower attached. Known as calorimeter poles, they were to record the intensity of heat as it spread in ever widening concentric circles. The time it took for the heat to reach them was noted, so that each emplacement had to be fixed in position relative to the future source. This was a complete project in itself involving much field work and many nightly calculations. I had been warned of the need for these in advance so when they arrived it was no surprise.

Meanwhile, back at the village area the all-weather air-strip had been finished and was at last in use. It looked quite impressive stretching out snow white along the side of the Claypan. The water distilling plants were still doing a brave job, battling with the salt bore water to provide our life-blood even though the pipes would fill with dried minerals and were repeatedly being hammered, removed, cleaned, and replaced to carry on. They could not stand idle for a day and the pipe bolts were worn smooth with the constant maintenance necessary. At the same time the taps in the ablutions were corroding rapidly as neat untreated bore water passed through them daily. However, we hoped they would all last until our job was finished.

The newspaper committee came up with a new idea—the production of a grand final edition of "Bulldust" to be distributed at the appropriate time with the Christmas cards. Sporting a coloured front page, achieved once again by Luke's silk screen method, the edition would be a summing up of the year's work. Although it would not be needed for some time, the men began work almost immediately. The first and most lengthy step was the production of about five hundred of the coloured covers to be stapled to the finished bundle of sheets. Luke once again prepared his utility office for the operation, and out came all the pots of coloured paints and the silk screen frame. I secured one of our standard covers for the Claypan newspaper, coloured it by hand with water paints, and despatched it to H.Q. to be photographed through filters.

In due course it was returned complete with negatives, and the screens were once more sensitized and set up for production. Meanwhile the editor collected all the material and prepared it for publication. The news items could not be completed until nearer the date for distribution, of course, but further stencilled drawings and selected items could be handled as well as extracts of special interest from previous editions. I suppose it could be called "Late Final Extra"—the difference being that whereas the paper boys meant late in the day, we meant late in the year. Later, in the homes of the scientists in England, I noticed copies of the result of our efforts, carefully preserved in cabinets probably for them to browse through in the years to come as a reminder of their trip to the Claypan.

Throughout these incidental jobs for the community the volume of work on the project was never reduced. Planes and trucks still maintained a steady flow to Emu, bringing equipment needed and hauling goods, such as fuel and food which were being used constantly and therefore needed replacing.

At the foot of the tower a large engine bedded down on a concrete base and held firmly by strong bolts, was installed complete with a cotton-reel type winch drum and several hundred feet of steel cable. Its purpose was to hoist the bomb in a cradle to the top of the tower when all was ready. The cradle on a small railway type trolley would be wheeled out under the centre-line through the tower, and the cable attached running to a pulley at the top of the structure and back down to the winch on the engine. This would be started, put in gear, and as the slack was taken up, the atomic bomb would be *gently* raised to the peak where holding bolts would be ready to be inserted into the holes. The weapon would then be joined to cables by a team safely in possession of their master key out of Maddock's panel, and after the bomb received its final pat on the top for luck, the team would quickly descend the steps to their waiting vehicle. Unfortunately at this stage in the proceedings, the engine could not be removed and was left to come to whatever grisly end was in store for it. I didn't think it would even be hurt much to the amazement of the scientists who did nothing to enlighten me. I would see for myself when the time came.

Haircuts were being requested in increasingly more accurate styles about this time as the boys could see a possible end in view. Although there was still much to do, they figured hair wouldn't grow back to normal overnight. Even the rugged bulldozer fitter with his black hair impregnated with daubs of axle grease was getting more particular, washing it in dieseline before coming for his "Adelaide in seven weeks trim." McWilliams still wanted his survey trim, however, as he didn't have much left on his brown shiny head and Professor Titterton, a nuclear physicist from Sydney, still came for his usual "atom" trim. So did Sir William. By this time there was an absolute paddock of hair paving the ground outside my tent, but luckily another member of the camp fetched his clippers and eased the situation considerably.

Under Luke's tender care, the Tumbling Tommies were still coping adequately with the camp's sanitation both at the village and the forward area. There had been no health worries of any sort in the camp, nor had there been any casualties of real importance throughout the job to date, and with the various blasting operations and high level tower work that were carried out this was perhaps surprising.

One motor mechanic, Roy, had worked diligently on the task of restoring one of the utility trucks to normal after its long constant use by Ken Garden. It was now ready for a road test. As he drove along the helicopter road his front wheel hooked over a windrow left by the grader maintaining the surface, he lost control of the steering, and the vehicle overturned, coming to rest completely upside down on its cab roof. Roy was not hurt but for days afterwards he was the object of many good-humoured jokes. One, in the form of a cartoon, was cut from a

Under Luke's tender care, the Tumbling Tommies were still coping . . . .

magazine and pinned to the workshop notice board. It showed a small car in a similar position, still occupied by two elderly ladies one of whom had been driving. The words under the drawing read, "I'm sure there is a way out of this Edith—as I've seen Christmas beetles do it." Of course "Roy" was substituted for Edith.

While some routine jobs were easing with the relief from the pressure brought to bear upon them for so long, others were stepping up and getting into high gear for the finish. These were mainly the scientific sections of the work—the installation of equipment in the now finished block houses, the underground concrete emplacements nearer to the scene of the blast, and the wiring of recording instruments and cameras to the main system. Everything was running like clockwork as huge pieces of electronic equipment were manoeuvred with less than inches to spare, into feet-thick concrete housings. There had been absolutely no room for error on anyone's part from start to finish.

One of the most appropriate cartoons cut from a periodical and pasted in the mess ante-room happened to be drawn by a good artist friend of mine, Norman Hetherington, with whom I had gone to school and who since leaving had been on the art staff of a well-known Sydney magazine. His particular version of our situation at Emu showed two men—obviously scientists—wearing long white coats and glasses standing at an ordinary kitchen sink. There were piles of glass apparatus around, and while one was elbow deep in suds with his long sleeves rolled up, the other had a tea towel and a frown. "I've *had* these nuclear experiments," he was saying. "There's too much washing up."

12

Wider Field of Operations

It was now time to carry on with some of the work which, although unscheduled at the beginning, had arisen during the course of the year. In most urgent need of attention was the access road to the site from Mabel Creek. We had built it direct to the Claypan from Tallaringa Well, but as the bomb sites and radioactive Kittens layout areas were surveyed in their respective positions, this road had already become contaminated with the smaller nuclear trigger trials cutting across it. Before long the main bomb tower and a great radius around it would become much more dangerous and in fact would be screened off where the instruments indicated and declared a prohibited area to all. Everyone knew the deadly effects of atomic radiation on humans, and would not venture near at any price.

We had overcome the problem of the "hot" Kittens area by immediately diverting the incoming trucks past the camera D tower and along a special road we had computed and bulldozed into the area, once again tapping the helicopter road. It had meant extending this access with the bulldozer and grader to cut the original access, and erecting a large danger sign and detour sign across it. Anyone coming overland would therefore finish up at the village along the all-weather access to Area A, by-passing Kittens altogether. When the main bomb exploded, however, a complete new end for the road would have to be planned. On inspection of the map of the project, which I had been constantly keeping right up to date as the work progressed, I found the route was clear. We would carry on past the already made road to Camera C tower at the far end of Coronation

Parade and gradually swing around so that the new road was well clear of any future likely "hot" spot; then we would join again to the Mabel Creek access, where a barricade would be built and the same warning signs erected.

Before this could be commenced, some incidentals were needed near the testing site. For instance, for the tests for the rockets shooting through the radioactive mushroom cloud a large battery of rockets was to be placed on a spot diagonally through the bomb tower from an untouched section of the country, clear of any other instrumentation or road. When the bomb exploded and the mushroom was about to form, an electronic timer actuated once again by Maddock's single button, would begin firing them off through the boiling mass to fall in the clear area and be subsequently studied with geiger counters by a team wearing protective suits. The job of placing this battery fell upon me with relative suddenness making me silently thank heaven and myself that I had laid such a careful tight network of trig survey over everything in the first place, ignoring comments about the need for speed in other directions. It now merely meant selecting the clearest most suitable place for the rockets to land, using figures supplied about the range, previously tried, of the missiles themselves; with a series of calculations I could put in a peg, over which the battery trailer was to be placed in the thick bush; by these calculations the rockets could be made to land just where required. A short 'dozed access road to the peg would complete my part of this phase.

An official documentary film section from the U.K. headquarters had arrived with a task of securing a movie record of the project for a more complete record of the event, and they asked me to re-enact my first entry into this location to put at the opening of the film. By the time they had finished I had some idea of what goes on in Hollywood. In the first place I was not allowed to shave for a fortnight. Then I had to drive my Land Rover through the thickest mulga patch we could find, stop in a mulga clearing, climb out dressed in rags (made filthy by rolling in a patch of dust), and look skywards, as if I wondered whether the sun was shining. Seeing that it was I had to unload my theodolite tripod, attach the instrument, consult my watch and some books, and carry out a sun observation. That completed, I was to do the fastest calculation for a sun latitude observation ever known to surveyor or mariner alike, plot it on a map and flop down on the sand, then boil a billy and make a cup of tea. The "nice cup of tea" was their idea.

Again at first light the next morning I had to spring out of my swag, make a fire, smash off a mulga stick, and stir a billy of porridge with it. It was all good fun and when I saw the finished film afterwards at H.Q. in Salisbury, I was amazed to see that with their skill, it had turned out better than I had expected.

Some of the maze of wires and cables were again being molested by dingoes at the more out-of-the-way sites with disastrous result, so some poison baits were laid to keep them at bay. A genuine gloom fell over the whole camp when Mick's faithful shadow dog, Pat fell victim to one. Pat had been a part of the camp and constant companion to Mick for the past six months. But one night she lay quietly outside Mick's tent instead of under his stretcher, her head cradled on her forepaws. At Mick's approach, she feebly moved her tail and within a short time had closed her eyes for the last time. He had been returning from the kitchen with his usual juicy bone for her supper when it happened, and no amount of salt and water or treatment had any effect. Mick broke down completely, and seemed in a daze as he got his Rover and a shovel and gently lifted Pat on to the passenger's seat and drove away slowly to a sandhill on his own to bury her. Throughout the entire period at Emu, this was the only tragedy.

When it was noticed that a security member burnt the paper napkins after each meal at Sir William's and Professor Titterton's table, the boys inevitably decided to play a joke on him. At the conclusion of most meals, the two scientists would have an earnest discussion over the table, often demonstrating some obscure point with a pencil on the nearest paper available—the paper napkins. Since everything was top secret in the eyes of the security section, one officer would await their departure, pounce on the paper covered in weird hieroglyphics, and burn the evidence. He was doing what any alert security officer should do, but the boys being what they were hit upon a plan which for once needed no committee. The fewer who knew about it the better. One obtained a collection of mathematical signs and symbols from books and friends, and wrote them up in a meaningless array of pseudo complicated calculations around a small drawing on a paper napkin. He clearly marked a rubber-stamped TOP SECRET sign on the top edge and placed it apparently carelessly in the security officer's waste paper basket in his office. When the officer saw it he leapt at it, opened it hurriedly, quickly folded it, and made at once for Sir William's tent to ascertain if it were of any importance before destroying it. Sir William, after a short examination of it, noticed the small inscription written alongside the drawing among the integral signs, and read it out loud. "Formula for," he began, "the making of a radioactive tin opener." Even the security officer burst into peals of uncontrollable laughter.

I considered I could make a better job of the deviation to the Tallaringa access road if I had a quick look over it from the air first, so I asked if I could go to Woomera in a York and return on another the same day. The pilots readily agreed and offered me the co-pilot's seat in the cabin, where I was hoping that I could take my eyes off the dozens of instruments long enough to make my air recce. I explained on a map where I wanted to go (which of course was on their way back anyway) and why, before donning a leather pilot's cap with built-in earphones and mike. I was careful to keep my hobnailed boots clear of the pedals and, shirtless in the heat of the cabin, leant back to observe the take-off procedure.

After checking several thousand things off a list the sergeant fitter started the engines and worked the four throttle levers forward a fraction. I was wondering when the pilot was going to do something, for until now he had just sat there listening. Finally, he condescended to place a flying boot on each pedal, let off the brakes, and steer the huge aircraft to the take-off end of the strip as the sergeant favoured first one set of engines and then the others in succession increasing the revs to keep the aircraft from turning. With the aircraft in position and the all-weather strip stretching out in front, each engine was run up in turn, again by the sergeant, who checked each set of instruments. When he was satisfied he gave a thumbs up sign to the pilot who at last held on to the stick as the sergeant once more edged the four throttle levers forward with one hand, still studying the instrument panel. As we gathered speed I just had to look ahead to see where we were going. It seemed to me the pilot's job was the most relaxed one aboard as he eased back on the stick to cause this monster to soar into the sky. This time he did not fly over our lines of tents but banked and headed for Camera C. Once the craft was airborne the hard-working sergeant again took over spinning the automatic pilot screws and working levers until the pilot himself let go everything and reclined in his seat. I thought that I could have done as much as he did to get it into the air but at the critical point of take-off I was not so sure and was glad he was there after all.

In another minute we were at Camera C and from then on I took more interest in the sandhill pattern. Making notes and sketching on a map across my knees I finished up with all I needed for my project; I mentioned this fact over the intercom, and we headed for Mabel Creek. Throughout the flight there I noticed where I could improve the access and noted it all on my map. This was the easiest survey reconnaissance I had ever done, and all from a soft leather armchair.

Ten miles north of Mabel Creek was another homestead, Mount Clarence where Charlie Kunoth lived and as he was also a particularly good friend the pilot asked if I would like to fly over his house. I readily agreed and the sergeant released the auto-pilot and the real one took over. Within a minute's detour we were over Charlie's brand new homestead on which he had been working. As we looked down we saw old Charlie amble outside to see the low-flying plane not realizing that I was aboard; we banked and flew lower and lower until we were not much more than windmill height over him as we screamed past. I could imagine Charlie, a real outback character saying to himself "by cripes" as his ten gallon hat blew off. Naturally, I resolved to tell him about it later when I finished up with the 'dozers at Mabel Creek.

We flew back to Emu that afternoon, and that night I finalized arrangements started by the team picked for the job. Once more, with rolled swag and billy, we set off in the morning. With the help of my air recce map we left Camera C, bulldozing almost from the foot of the tower, and in two days had formed a new loop to join the original road in, well clear of any area that was likely to be contaminated in the future. When we met up with it, "Chook" Fowler, driving the old D7, heaped up a barrier of dirt, blocking off the Claypan section of the old road for ever, and "Nugget" driving the worn D8 machine with "Hekyll" following in the grader carried on with me to our old Dingo Claypan which had been Bill Lloyd's and my starting point for the whole thing, a year before. We had planned to join up the two Claypans with a twenty odd mile road as part of this operation, and it was the only time any of us had seen Hekyll and Jekyll apart for six months.

Everything was hard including the ground we slept on until we passed by Tallaringa Well. Nevertheless, things went quickly and smoothly. We had at last joined the Claypans for future work and had completed the deviation loop. The first hint of trouble came when one of the anchorages for the arms of the blade of the D7 finally tore away leaving it swinging in mid-air. Chook had immediately stopped the machine and we dragged the blade back into position with the same logging winch of the D8 that had pulled the bumper-bar clean off the bogged tip-truck months before. Holding it in place we tied a loose reef knot with a huge piece of steel blade lift cable from the D7 that went right around both separated units, and pulled it tight by driving off into the bush on the grader with the free end attached. That put that machine out of commission for use as a bulldozer but it could be driven now with the heavy blade lashed up to take the A frame over the radiator. The other machine would do whatever else was needed with its usable blade.

We had no sooner come to the end of the improvements on my map that I had noted from the air, when a loud knocking started up from somewhere inside the tremendous engine of the D8. The fitter examined it and declared if we were lucky we might sneak it the rest of the thirty miles into Mabel Creek slowly on one pair of cylinders less, which meant the end of the blade work for either. Fortunately we had just finished anyway. In this way with the grader ahead brushing over and smoothing our first road made by Smokey, we limped into Mabel Creek and switched off all the plant for the last time that year.

I drove up the ten miles to see Charlie Kunoth to tell him about the place and listen to the yarns he was always ready to tell. This time he was full of the "coot that flew over and nearly knocked me windmill over." I quickly told him that I was aboard and he laughed until he cried. If the mill had been knocked over it would not have worried Charlie a bit; he would have simply put it up again.

I finally got a chance to ask him about something that I had seen outside the new house as I drove up. There on the windswept open gibber and saltbush paddocks was his solid new masonry homestead all painted and fresh, while just outside he still had his old tin garage with the loose iron flapping and creaking in the wind, housing his gleaming latest model American car. Apparently three years before when I had promised to design him a sundial from a star observation that I had taken outside his old place, I had placed a pencilled arrow on a windowsill of his old garage as a reference mark to line it up when it was ready. The sundial was to be an ornament on a rock pedestal to go with his future new house. I had been amazed to hear from him that he had remembered there was something important about that window sill, so he had refused to allow the builders to touch it until the sundial was in place. I had been so constantly in the bush since the star observation night that although I had calculated it along with the divisions for the shadow readings I had not been in the town long enough to find a suitable engraver to make it for us.

I was pleased my reference mark was still there as it would save a further set of figures when I did find time to install the sundial, but at the same time I wondered how many bushmen would have

Even with his sundial, old Charlie still relied on his grandfather clock

given that detail a second thought, especially as the builders were right on the spot. Good old Charlie. I resolved there and then to have it made over Christmas in Adelaide and bring it back myself, a resolution that I carried out.

Charlie asked me if I could mend his new grandfather clock. He complained that it struck ten when it read nine o'clock and so on, which meant that he had got out of bed an hour earlier for a week until he discovered it. "I used to sit here and wait for it to read six o'clock," he told me, "and while it was striking seven I tried whizzing the hands round to seven before it stopped." He explained it would still read eight as it struck nine times so he gave up winding the chimes. I was able to make the time on the face correspond with the chimes by removing the hands and putting them back an hour later. Charlie pushed back his ten-gallon hat. "By cripes" he said, "never thought of that."

You could never be sure whether Charlie was pulling your leg. But I strongly suspected he was when I heard the amazing story of his visit to Adelaide to select the new furniture for the finished mansion. According to him he sat in a comfortable chair and wrote cheques as his wife bought everything on her own. When they had finished their purchases he discovered that they wouldn't fit on the lorry he had driven down, so he promptly went along and bought a new and larger one. Asked if he had one to trade in, he replied as if he'd just remembered "Yeah, by cripes, it's parked outside one of them big furniture shops somewhere." While they were loading on the carpets by the acre, he had been looking at a tool they were lending him to lay it himself. It was a flattened iron shaft, with vertical spikes at one end, and a large soft leather pad at the other. They assured him that it would make the laying a simple matter. He asked the shop assistant how he knew that he was going to get a blackfeller to help him. The unfortunate and bewildered city shop worker looked at him blankly wondering what he was talking about until old Charlie gave his version of what this special tool was used for. "I'll nail it down around the edges as the blackfeller drags it out tight," he explained, "and by cripes if he gets too slow I'll dong him on the head with the knob to hurry him up." Before the shop man doubled up, Charlie continued grimly, "and if that doesn't do the trick, by cripes I'll use the other end."

When we finished fixing the clock, he informed me that he didn't like the tune the chimes played, so at his insistence I bent the striking arms, but could still only get the first four notes of Walzing Matilda on it for him. I always enjoyed seeing Charlie, and felt reluctant when it was time to leave him. But there was work to be done so I waved and returned to Mabel Creek and the boys who were now ready to return on our improved road to the Claypan.

There was a Peace Officer camped by the station. He was on duty all the time, stopping every car to check for possible undesirables furtively seeking information about the atomic project (this was the only junction with the main road into Emu). Normally he would have been lucky to see one car a day, but right then somebody was holding a half-way around Australia car trial in which vehicles with impatient drivers would come rocketing along to keep up with their tight schedules. That made no difference as far as our security went, as anybody could be posing as a trials driver, and arrange a convenient breakdown in his tortured car at Mabel Creek. Our Peace Officer had orders to stop every moving conveyance of any kind, check it thoroughly, and enter names and numbers in his book as well as the time they were there, with the result that the already tried and harassed drivers were transformed into fuming savage wild men actually foaming at the mouth with the unexplained delay. But they did not worry the Peace Officer as, in his slow, meticulous way he went through their papers, oblivious to the sounds of blaring horns when several arrived at once. It occurred to me that all these precautions only served to draw more attention to the fact that something big was on here.

I went over to ask the Peace Officer if there was anything he needed or any message that he would like to pass on to Emu. He was in touch by radio but he still might be out of some rations we could give him from our supply before we returned. While we were talking, a group of four cars roared down the road, throwing up so much dust that I wondered how the drivers of the ones in the rear could see at all. They skidded to a stop behind each other at his wooden barrier across the road. Slowly standing up from his stretcher and carefully adjusting his cap, the officer reached for his book and pencil and together we walked towards the waiting cars. The drivers were anxious to get going as the officer carefully studied their papers. Their cars all showed signs of the punishment that they had been receiving; rattling mudguards were held on with fencing wire, and rope and bits dragged along the ground behind. Many windscreens had been shattered by stones thrown up, and the drivers, who had bashed gaping holes to enable them to see, were covered in a thick layer of red dust which entered the opening. They wore goggles to protect their eyes and had tied rags around their faces to make breathing possible. I wondered what induced men to put up with such discomfort just for pleasure. Although we did a similar sort of thing daily and the plant operators had the same appearance after each day on their machines, they didn't do it for fun— it was their job.

We left some extra tins of jam and our remaining bread with the officer, and began the long return journey out to the Claypan. The others headed off along the finished road while I came along last to save checking if they were still coming, hoping I would not fall by the wayside myself. After camping at Tallaringa, we resumed the trip to Emu. As the others in front came to our bulldozed barricades they turned for Camera C. I stopped to read the sign which had been painted and erected in our pile of dirt and branches across the road during our absence.

Although it would be easy to drive around the heap and on to the old road again, after reading the warning sign about deadly radiation, nobody in their right mind could even be induced to try. I jumped out, bare footed as often in the heat, to check on my tyres before continuing on to finish the trip to the village via Camera C. The place was alive with vehicles and men as they worked at the dozens of instrument installations for the event which now, with so little time left, seemed a reality.

My first task on arrival was to add the latest road deviation to my map of the area to bring it up to date. Even left for a week it would be an ancient historical document at the rate the place was progressing. After a welcome shower in the salty bath sheds, where I suspect my bluchers still had a familiar ring as they hit the concrete floor, and a change into a different shirt, I ate a good meal at a table instead of sitting in the sandhills, and felt a new person altogether. I was ready for a long sleep in my old swag—this time unrolled on top of a soft stretcher. . . .

13

Surveys for Remote Instrumentation

Immediately after the bomb explodes, the ground is covered with minute particles of radioactive dust which decrease in intensity and power as they settle further out. The degree of radiation varies with the proximity of the point of detonation, and if gauged, a contour plan can be drawn. The harmfulness of the invisible rays emitted from these microscopic particles diminishes rapidly after forming, first by the minute, then hourly, until the curve gradually tapers off. Apparently it is many decades before every vestige of contamination vanishes, although after a few years there is no longer any real risk to humans visiting the scene.

If a man lingered for seconds immediately after the fission had occurred, he could not survive. In half an hour a quick visit to the spot can be made providing the visitor is ready to evacuate the moment his mobile instruments advise that he has taken enough. On the following day, the bomb site can be checked by geiger counters and gamma ray monitors, as long as the operator keeps his eye on his "dosimeter"and wears the special suit designed for such work. A dosimeter is a fountain-pen-like tube containing a crystal and indicating mark. It is held up to the light of the sky and is used like a telescope, and when the indicating line actuated by radiation moves across the crystal to a danger mark, it is no longer safe to remain there. As well as the dosimeter, and as an added precaution, a small section of unexposed film is carried in a frame three feet from the ground or at about waist level, marked with the wearer's name. After each visit to the forward area a new one is supplied and the photographic section develops the square of film to observe whether it has been exposed to a danger level of radiation.

After each excursion to the future "hot spot" by the scientists, the goon suits were discarded in a special shed to be washed in our salt bore water laundry and the men were required to stand on a platform with their hands inserted into slots in an instrument panel. If a bell rang before the end of the measured time, during which the apparatus was switched on they had to have a second shower. One set of slots were vertical for one sort of ray test and another horizontal for the rest, and so delicate were the dials involved that one member was forced to have fourteen showers after each ringing of his bell before the attendants casually advised him to remove his luminous wrist watch.

The goon suit consisted of plain underclothing and silk overalls fastened securely at the back, with a double sleeve on each arm and two concentric tubes at the bottoms of the trouser legs. One sleeve was peeled back leaving the other held firmly at the wrist with elastic. A rubber seamless glove was put on to the elbow and the outer arm fabric was rolled down over the outside of the glove to the wrist, again held by a band. Rubber boots were worn on the feet and a large white bag, roughly foot-shaped, was tied right over the boot at the knee. To complete the picture a full face respirator was necessary to prevent the men breathing in dust particles thrown up by the vehicle; a white scarf reversed and tied at the back helped to seal off the neck opening, and a white skull cap prevented any contamination from particles lodging in the hair. It was quite an unforgettable experience to wear a goon suit in temperatures around the century for a day at a time. After this hands and fingers were converted into something resembling sweat-soaked bunches of prunes.

How far does this immediate ground radiation extend? How

far does one need to travel away from the hottest spot to be safe? What is the rate of deterioration of the fallout over a given period as against distance? All these questions have to be answered by actual controlled observations to make trials of this sort worth while. A series of readings taken hourly at fixed points and less frequently as the readings indicate are plotted on graphs and blank forms, and the result is a visual picture of the pattern and change of pattern of the R.H. (Radiation Hazards or Radio Health) contours for a bomb of the size being currently tested. These results can be used in cases of emergency where no instruments are available.

In order that the readings may be taken quickly, plotted accurately, and read and re-read on the same points for comparison, hundreds of points must be fixed in relation to the centre of the explosion beforehand. Before the weapon could be triggered, we had to decide on the direction of the ground wind to carry the bulk of the heavier particles away harmlessly to the sandhills. Then with this as a rough centre line, we devised a bulldozed grid network involving forty or fifty miles of bulldozed lanes resembling tennis racquet strings, designed to straddle it for the best readings. The lanes would not only show the operators of the instruments where the stamped labelled steel pegs were, but they would also provide a Land Rover access for quicker travel between readings. A steel peg was required every quarter of a mile along each lane and a sheaf of scale blank maps showing only the grid was reproduced for further filling in.

This was going to be a lengthy and tedious job, so, with the bulldozer and Mick and Blue to help, and with the previous night's calculations as a guide, we lumbered away on our mission, which was to take several weeks.

When our work was completed and we had proved our calculations correct, another stage of the trials came to light. This involved underground seismic shock waves which recorded how far and to what intensity ground disturbances could be expected. We had to do a series of remote astronomical observations with surveyed lines of instruments directed straight for the bomb tower.

I thought the stretcher and showers were too good to last so after rolling the swag once more I set out for the main seismic site at Tallaringa Well about seventy miles away as the crow flies.

I had been thinking a lot about that access road and how we had to go north from Camera C crossing seven miles of sand ridges, then recrossing them all again further east on the Tallaringa bound section of the original one; this was the only way in. I resolved to do a little extra recce survey on my own on this trip from our Camera C to discover if it would be practical to improve on the road location again. I could readily combine the two jobs on my way to do the star observations.

On reaching Camera C, I disregarded all the roads and plunged off into the bush, travelling east with the sandhills. Where a decision had to be made as to which side of a sand ridge fade-out to go, I invariably took the southern side; this way I was always heading for Tallaringa and saving one more crossing. Whereas when the first road in went directly to the Claypan itself, the subsequent development of the bomb site had made a change necessary. We had had to cope with it in a relative hurry, but now I knew that I should never be content until I had guided a bulldozer and grader over it to make it a fixture. There probably wouldn't be time this year for it, but there would be an opportunity one day. The change actually came about four years later and then I was glad that I had done the recce on this trip.

I was not surprised at the end of forty miles of scrub-bashing that there was still no evidence of the other road, so I decided to carry on the whole seventy miles if necessary, to reach Tallaringa by the best route. I'd already had two flat tyres that day in the bush, the last one half-way down a sandhill where I was forced to use my two tyre levers as a plate on the sand to prevent the jack from sinking out of sight in the soft surface. The country, as I already knew, was still covered by hundreds of sandhills, but for a change they at least ran in the direction I was travelling. Reduced once again to, or rather still in, my normal uniform of dusty rags held on with a belt, watch and penknife pouch, and bare feet in sand impregnated hobnailed boots, I grew suddenly very tired as the light was fading. I had only eaten part of a tin of bully beef all day and I was looking forward to a heated tin of stew and a mug of cocoa, so after pushing on to the limit with every yard requiring greater effort, I found a place to camp free from fallen mulga scrub and salt-bush roots.

I heard it as soon as I had switched off the engine. The tell-tale hiss of my third staked tyre for the day as the air slowly escaped. Feeling exhausted, I clomped around to the tool box to fetch the jack to place under the axle before it went right down. The pair of tyre levers were missing. I had driven off from my last flat tyre on the sandhill seven miles back, leaving them buried under a layer of sand; without them I had no hope of mending any of three tyres. There was only one thing to do—turn around immediately, back track myself using the headlights, and get as far as I could towards the lost levers until the sick tyre gave out altogether. I had never lost anything like this before in the bush, but even in my exhausted state, mind triumphed over matter and in a minute I was labouring back into the dark like a worn-out retriever dog.

It was rather like a game. As each hundred yards passed I wondered just how much further I would be able to go. At each fallen mulga I carefully edged the vehicle around if possible or backed over it, and with the half-way mark reached I began to feel a little light-headed. I might even get the whole way there. Five miles passed, then six; if the tyre gave out now I could trudge the rest of the way with my torch light. But with the tyre just holding its own (more than half-way flat) as I had carefully left the pencil-shaped sliver of wood which was the cause of it all in place as a stopper, the stars must have been my way and smiling because sure enough according to my recorded speedo mile readings, at seven miles a high sand ridge appeared in front of the headlights. In the gloom I recognized the bloodwood tree at the scene of my last flat tyre changing, so I left the vehicle on the flat ground, switched off, and went on up the sandhill with my torch. There by the tree were the footmarks and the impressions of circular rims and a half minute later I was once again in possession of my precious pair of tyre levers. It was just eleven o'clock at night. Returning really bone weary to the vehicle with my prize, I noticed the tyre had given up completely and was spread out all over the ground like a camel's foot. At last I could have my hot mug of cocoa as the evening by now was growing chilly, but I must have been getting more light-headed than I thought. I suddenly burst into uncontrollable laughter. I now remembered that I had taken out the jack seven miles away, and in my hurry to get back for the levers before the tyre went down, I had thrown out my swag into the darkened bush. It was still there.

Out came all the tyre mending tools, all but the levers which were well and truly out already, and I set to in a semi-coma to mend the three tyres, knowing that I would have to return along the tracks to my swag to enable me to sleep on the cold sand at all, providing I had the choice and did not fall asleep over the wheel first. This must have looked awfully silly to the hawks and bats moving about on their branches contented as always with nothing, and I decided never to use the descriptive word "batty" again. Compared with me, they had it made—that night, anyway. Midnight saw me laboriously pumping by hand—there was no plug compression model at the time—the four hundred and fifty strokes it took to inflate each mended tyre. I had a pressure gauge but after hundreds of mendings and countings I invariably found that was the number for this sort of sand tyre. I was sorely tempted in this case to stop at a few less, but sheer dogged determination had long since set in, and each tyre got its due number. With one in place on the vehicle and the other two in their racks, I packed up knowing this time *everything* was aboard as I had left the vehicle on the level clear ground when I had arrived.

The trip back was one of more leisurely pace as this seven mile stretch in the bush was becoming a highway in its own right. Besides, there was not that urgency and anxiety I had felt at eleven o'clock. Well before three o'clock in the morning I came to the end of my tracks and there large as life was my swag. I forgot about the stew and cocoa as I rolled out the swag where it was and pulled the canvas over myself. I fell asleep almost before I had finished pulling it up.

Next day, after a mug of cocoa at last, plus the stew, I pushed on—earlier than I had expected—and cut on to my original road in less than twenty miles. There I erected a stew tin signpost reading, "Emu roughly sixty miles . . . roughly." I was soon at Tallaringa where the seismic team was camped among an array of equipment waiting for the pegs to lay it down.

From the way they almost ran away as I climbed out of my tattered Rover, I concluded I must have looked a bit rugged after my beating, but they complied with my request, to save me effort, of radioing Emu that I had arrived safe and almost sound. My first thought was for their rations and they readily gave me the banquet of my life, on the spot. Bread and jam, some apples, soup and biscuits. I was so grateful that they almost wept.

When I had finished I set about ascertaining their requirements. The discussion centred on a row of pegs which aimed themselves right towards the bomb tower so far away through the bush. With delicate recorders any ground shock wave could be measured by them and a wealth of information would result. Before setting up my theodolite for the night's star work and unloading my worn calculation tables and books, I plodded over to the split drum bathtub, filled it with foul smelling well water, and had a bath alfresco style with the soaring eagles as interested onlookers. During the observing I was forced to ask the men to extinguish their fire, as the heat shimmer rising into that part of the sky made the stars viewed through the telescope resemble large wobbly white jellies instead of steady pinpoints. Meanwhile, the men shivered until I had finished. Most of the calculations had to be done next morning as I was too done in to do them immediately after the observation.

After they had driven their set of pegs securely into the ground under the watchful cross wires of the theodolite, I headed once again back towards the Claypan, this time sticking to the made road. As I waved to the seismologists, I little dreamt what a nightmare this trip was to turn into. The outward journey seemed like a quiet Sunday afternoon drive in comparison.

The first hint of trouble came when on a good stretch the vehicle slowed from fifteen to five miles per hour. Thinking the hand brake had flicked on or the water was going from a possible turned on drain plug in the radiator, I checked but they were in order. I shrugged it off and carried on still at only five miles per hour; nothing I could do with gears or accelerator would induce the Rover to go a fraction faster. With sixty miles to cover this was going to take some time. I had passed my stew tin signpost by now, carefully looking the other way as I did so. Memories were still too fresh.

My thoughts turned to a sticky brake shoe then to a possible leak of differential oil, let out by some harder than usual contact between the brass drain plug and a log or stump. This would be slowly seizing up the gears as had happened to me once before in the bush. Leaping out to see, I found it dry and shiny and all in order, as were the brake shoes checked by jacking up each wheel in turn and hand spinning it. Off once again at five miles per hour until an amazing thing happened. On a clear, harder section of the road the engine suddenly revved itself up and I was off at twenty in seconds. Pleased that the crawling was over I carried on until without warning back it went to five. Electrical now. I jumped out after switching on the lights and sure enough they were just glimmering weakly. Looking over the engine wiring wishing that I were Maddock or Frank Hill, I couldn't discover a thing wrong or even a loose connection. Off again at five. In this way, fluctuating up and down at will, the vehicle stumbled along.

I comforted myself with the thought that the boys could handle this, and if they despaired old Barnie would find the trouble with his eyes shut. With forty miles left to go a front spring gave out altogether, so I simply tied the broken half of the assembly out in front with fencing wire. This was to be almost my undoing, because when a rear spring also went, the vehicle mudguards at the rear came to rest on the tyre stopping forward motion; now friction took over and the tyre smelled strongly of burning rubber. As I walked around the front to get my axe for chopping off a mulga branch to act as a solid chock to free the tyre, I had forgotten about the spring jutting out in front shin-high from the ground. As I ran into it I came as close as ever I want to come to breaking my leg. I fell down in agony, nursing the leg with both hands but later tentatively exploring the damage, all I could find apart from a bleeding slice across my leg was a huge swollen lump. I struggled up using the spring as a lever and hobbled on to get the axe. Chopping a length of mulga from a sitting position is not the easiest thing to do but finally with the vehicle jacked off the tyre the chock was in place and twitched on with the usual wire. The leg was feeling as if I had been tortured for a week by now. Luckily it wasn't the accelerator and brake leg.

Away once more fluctuating like fury, but at least mobile, and in a few miles I thought that I could carry on to make it back to camp. With all this delay the afternoon had passed by and it was dusk once again, but like Luke I decided to carry on to get this ordeal over. How naïve I was. Soon it was quite dark, and when the vehicle slowed to five miles per hour and the headlights dimmed, I could barely see anything, so, after the night's star work, I lashed my torch, fitted with new batteries, to the front grille adjusting it on a wheeltrack a little in front of the car and crawled it along with my head out of the window trying to see where I was going. When the vehicle decided to go at twenty I would jump out or rather limp out to switch off the torch as the headlights were with me once more during these bursts. Once I looked into the darkened engine to see if sparks from an electrical short were in evidence but not a sign. After all there were only about twenty-five miles to go to Camera C and fifteen more to the village.

Fate seemed to be against me. I had my head out of the window studying the road by the dimming torch light, when suddenly, out of the corner of my eye, I saw something reflecting off the window. It was a bright glow in the gloom as Frank Hill would have put it, and its source was a tongue of flame a foot long coming from the hub of the rear wheel. "Oh no, not that, anything but that," I mumbled as I moved faster than I felt like on my aching leg to grab handfuls of loose dirt and fling it over the fire as fast as I could before it took hold. With all the instruments, maps, and field books on the vehicle I just couldn't afford to have a burnt-out car, sore leg or not. The fire out, I hastened to fill a billy with water from my tank to cool down the heated steel and prevent it from bursting into flames again as the thick black axle oil seeped out over the rim on to the dirt. In spite of being in quite a state at the thought of losing the vehicle which, with its cargo, was worth as much as half a dozen vehicles, I remembered to switch off the engine and the torch which I unlashed. Then I studied the disaster area closely. The wheel bearing had been chewed to pieces breaking the leather seals, and the oil had been allowed to seep out rapidly, filling up the now binding brake shoe in the drum. Eventually the friction produced had caused it to catch fire. I knew then that I'd had it, like the scientists with the washing up, and accepted defeat.

In other circumstances I would have wound bits of my belt around the thing with the hope of making a leather bearing or doing *something* anyway, but in this case it was too late for that. I rigged up my radio transceiver aerial, contacted the ever alert control room to explain my position and plight, and asked for the tow truck wrecker to come out and drag me back. They replied that they would certainly come out that night for me and in due course the glow of their *bright* headlights appeared on the horizon. It was only half-past two in the morning when my Rover and I both limped into camp. I'd had precious little sleep and food for three days and nights now, but the first aid man insisted on working on my leg as I ate a huge lump of fruit cake brownie made ready by Ozzie. Then I crawled to my tent.

Next morning or nearer midday a security officer appeared at my stretcher side in a great state of agitation. He told me they'd discovered a bare footprint at the junction of the detour road from Camera C and the original access. Everyone concerned in the camp was in a near panic, convinced that some unsuspecting nomadic natives were ambling about in danger. In spite of my leg and hunger, I burst out laughing. When I could speak I explained to the astonished officer that the track belonged to me; that I had jumped out bare footed after reading the sign to check my tyres as we returned from Mabel Creek with Hekyll, Nugget, and Chook. I was still laughing as was he, when I turned over and went back to sleep, leaving him to hurry off to relieve the tension in the camp.

When I got up during the afternoon I discovered somebody had got the story wrong about the mulga chock with which I had propped up the car over the differential. Weary Willie told me that he had heard I had been in trouble last night "but I was okay as I'd made a spare differential out of mulga wood." I told him casually that I had used a handful of white ants in place of the oil which had all drained away. Wide-eyed he hurried off to give out this latest bit of news to the community.

While over at the workshops seeing the mechanics, who had descended on my Rover in force, at work, I noticed a grader driver I hadn't seen for many months, standing by his machine waiting for some help. I went to him asking where he'd been all this time. "I got crook"—he'd obviously told his story many times—"and they flew me away to hospital." I told him that I hadn't heard about it, so he went on, "They went and hacked open me guts"—he outlined the incision marks with a dusty finger traced over his abdomen in the shape of a six inch cross—"and they peeled back the four bits, pulled out somethin', fixed 'er up, an' shoved it all back in." I was finding it a job to keep a straight face as he concluded his most graphic description of the delicate operation "they" had performed on him. "Then they dragged back the bits," he said "and sewed 'em all back on to each other again real strong." He made the surgeons sound more like medieval blacksmiths with every word and I was forced to withdraw to the other side of my Rover.

There seemed an air of something about to happen in the mess that night as I hobbled in for tea. I was soon to discover the cause. Suddenly John Tomblin stood up to announce Sir William had something to say, and I had the strange feeling that everyone except me knew already. And that was the case; he asked me to come over, made a little speech of thanks for my help to his English team on this project, and presented me with an engraved tankard from the Englishmen. I was overcome and could only say in reply to his doubts as to what I was going to use it for that it would be ideal for my cocoa . . . I would even be able to see if there were any ants in it through the glass bottom. I was very touched by their thought, and the tankard immediately became my most prized possession from the Claypan.

I had been hearing a word like "rontchen" bandied about for weeks, and finally asked Vere Stupart, the expert of the coaxial cable and associated instrumentation fame, what it meant. He smiled as he explained the word was Röntgen meaning the fundamental unit by which atomic radiation is measured, and impressed upon me it was pronounced "Rönt-gen" with the "g" hard as in golf. I wondered if perhaps he might be growing just a little homesick at last.

14

Start of Reconnaissance for a New Permanent Site

Without warning or hint of any kind, a new and really big plan had been made and was already taking shape at the various H.Q. involved in the overall defence research programme. I had been vaguely wondering what might become of this testing site in the future after it had become contaminated, but up to now there had not been much time for thought about anything beyond the present. Even the Whip was finding he could start relaxing and climbing off many backs and he was rapidly becoming well liked and respected by the men who were beginning to realize that he was only carrying out his tremendous job well and with efficiency. Luke was adding to his collection of water-colour pictures of the camp. Ken Garden was often to be seen joking, Mountain Lowrey and Flip Woolley were in the highest of spirits and Chinny McWilliams just continued at the top peak which he had maintained throughout. Lorry Hogan had even time to learn an encore to "Nut Brown Maiden" on the bagpipes, while old Barnie Bentley was taking longer and longer to get his eyes open after once closing them to diagnose trouble in some engine or other. Sir William and Professor Titterton were scribbling on fewer paper napkins, and the hard-working plane unloading team were finding there wasn't much to unload. All around the camp was to be felt an atmosphere of relief from routine and strain, together with excited anticipation of the tremendous and historic event in which everyone had had a hand and which was almost at our threshold.

One day a different sort of aircraft flew over the camp, landed

161

on the all-weather runway, and taxied to the unloading bay where some passengers alighted. I was pleased to see our friends Alan Butement, the Chief Scientist, in charge of Australia's Defence Science which includes Woomera, and George Pither, the Range Superintendent among them, and hastened over to greet them. A long time had elapsed since our first combined visit to Dingo Claypan and Area A, and after an enthusiastic exchange of salutations I was introduced to the other passengers. Apparently I was known to them already, although I just couldn't place them at the moment. One was a Wing-Commander in the R.A.A.F., Kevin Connolly, a rugged well-built outdoor type with a swarthy face and ready, friendly smile. He was clutching an obviously prized possession—a beautifully engraved double-barrelled twelve-gauge shotgun, complete with a silver shield inscribed and let in to the glass-like polished butt. He carried it as any one else might carry a brief case. He was an engineering officer concerned with modifications to aircraft.

The next one named Beavis was a very likeable younger man of taller build, slim, full of fun and an expert on soil chemistry and the various treatments needed for airfield construction.

The other was a pilot with the R.A.A.F. whom I did remember, Flight-Lieutenant Charles Taplin, who had not only flown me on various survey flights but also sported a huge horizontal moustache. He had twinkling eyes always ready for a joke, and his own style of describing anything he saw. I remembered once that he had called a small, newly scratched out area of dust we had noticed in the bush "A kangawoo's vamping pit." He was also a very careful but otherwise unorthodox pilot, ignoring his navigator's plotted bearings and flying where he thought he should go. One baffled navigator, trying to keep a plot of where the aircraft was at all times, trailed off and wrote across the log, "I give up." That must have been when Charlie was swooping low and banking from one side to the other in order to obtain a better view of a mob of "kangawoos."

With the party had arrived three brand new Land Rovers, stacked full of camping gear, radio transmitting equipment, ration boxes, and water containers. I was still just a little in the dark about all this, but I was rapidly getting the feeling this operation included me in some way, and as I looked over the shiny new billies and equipment I was already saying goodbye again to the shower rooms and stretcher. How right I was. I was soon to be on a five hundred mile reconnaissance survey expedition through virgin bush and sandhills, salt lakes and horizons of open plains. Not that I was not always ready for an exploration with my swag rolled for the fray, but a solid year of it without much let up both night and day was tending to make me feel just a little haggard.

That afternoon I was called down to Sir William's tent where he, Alan, and Luke were sitting about on camp chairs. I took a place on a stretcher. George, Kevin, Beavis, and Charlie were busy at the Rovers reorganizing their loads, replenishing water and petrol containers, and seeing that their vehicles were being serviced to be in tip-top order.

Alan Butement said that it had been decided that a more permanent test site was required. Safety studies had shown that it could be nearer to the railway, so saving thousands of flying hours, fuel, and so on. He intended to lead a recce party himself to find a suitable site, and wished me to come along to survey the route. This idea was the outcome of many high-level negotiations—both international and Federal. The railway concerned was the Transcontinental Line across six hundred miles of the bare uninhabited Nullarbor Plain. This line lay two hundred miles to the south of Emu with entirely uninhabited country in between. A site roughly south of Emu would be the same straight-line distance to Woomera as it was from Emu itself, with a shorter route to Adelaide. It would also have the added advantages of reducing the cost of hauling hundreds of tons of freight on the goods trains, and giving direct telephone link to the outside world instead of relying on radio alone. This would be done by adding a further set of wires to the existing poles along the line which would be handled in a most pleasant, quiet, and efficient way by the divisional P.M.G. engineer in Adelaide, Don Burnard also a great friend of mine.

Although I had no way of knowing it at the time, we were in fact, sitting there calmly discussing the beginning of what was to develop into the multi-million pound project to be known as the Maralinga permanent atomic weapons testing range for British trials in Australia. The results of the present trials at Emu would have by then added much to the knowledge of the behaviour of the bomb, and the layout of the new proposed site would benefit from the experiences gained there.

So that was it. Back to the swag, billycan, and quietness of deserts, mulga, and salt lakes. Sir William Penney agreed that my work here was fully done—not that he'd consider having me miss the final Emu explosion. But there was time enough left to carry out the expedition on which I would do the star observations necessary to ensure that we got through, and complete the survey and bush-bashing with my reinforced vehicle now completely restored by the workshops team under good old Captain George Johnstone.

George Pither had already carried out an extensive air reconnaissance of the suggested areas, from which trip as well as his notes had emerged an excellent sketch map, defined at the Department of the Interior survey section above his office in Woomera by Aubrey Guy. Not long before Aub Guy's sudden and tragic death from a heart attack, he and I had between us drawn the designs for the menu used at the official dinner given on the occasion of the Duke of Edinburgh's visit to the Woomera Rocket Range.

It was going to take me a short time to organize the instruments needed and to push them into any crevice available between the vehicle tins of emergency rations. I knew only too well

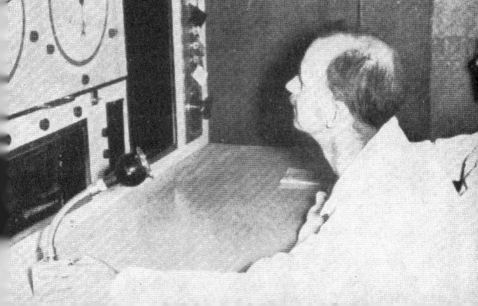

what such a trip was going to involve. At least there would be four vehicles against my usual one.

The party had arranged that we be accompanied by two huge three-ton trucks loaded with food, fuel, and water, but I suggested they might be more of an encumbrance than help to us, as I was sure they would get bogged at the first sandhill. We agreed however to try them to see how far they could get. If they stopped we could transfer everything from them to our vehicles and carry on while they returned to Emu. (Actually they only went four and a half miles.) A light aeroplane also was flown in by Peter Campbell, a Squadron-Leader from Woomera, to be stationed at Emu. From there it could supply us, on radio request, with any vital mechanical part we required. It would also facilitate our choice of route.

In addition to this support—something I had never known before on a bush-bashing trek—heavier aircraft were held ready for instant take-off at Woomera. George arranged that they were to be loaded with cardboard "storepedoes" and parachutes for dropping supplies big or small to us when asked for. They could navigate to us from astrofixes I would supply, and we could indicate the last detail by smoke generators and flares. I found myself rather looking forward to this trip, tired though I was and hard as it was undoubtedly going to be.

At this stage my first concern was for the Rovers, so I headed off for Barnie and the workshops where the others were working as well. Looking over their gear I found that no one seemed to have a properly shaped tyre lever, and as this was one of the most used requirements, I said I would make several on the anvil from broken springs to my own well-tried design. I had forged up two, oil-tempered them, and was on the third when it happened. One end of the spring was a bright cherry red from the forge; I was holding the other by tongs made slightly slippery by sump oil. As I brought the hammer down on the spot I wanted to taper off, the whole thing somehow slipped out of the tongs. It reared up end on to my left armpit to leave a searing cut from the glowing steel under my old shirt which had burnt through instantly. The pain was terrific on that soft part, but only momentarily, then acute throbbing set in; at this stage there was not much bleeding because of the cauterizing action of the red hot end. In spite of it all I had to laugh a little as I recalled my idea of the grader driver's description an hour or so before of the medieval blacksmith's "surgeon's" methods, rather similar to these. Kevin had seen the incident and rushed over, but I managed to burn the oil from the beaks of the tongs in the fire and finish off the lever before the first aid sergeant came to patch it up. I went with him to the hut assuming that there were at least no germs alive in the wound.

Bright and early next morning we again rolled our swags, had a big drink of water, and set off once more from Emu village. I carried some extra salve and bandage for my now very sore but special souvenir wound.

This was where the turn-off I had made seemingly an age ago to the Kittens was to act as a permanent indication of our exact lead-out tracks. After a quiet study of George's map and all the other maps I had in my tent late at night, I had decided it would be best to head the party off into the bush from this point. The reason for this was that when the light aircraft came to make its flights out to us from Emu, it could start off along the Kittens road at little more than tree top height and when this road terminated at the helicopter road, Peter could carry straight on, following our fresh wheeltracks until he reached us. Before leaving I carefully informed Pete of this intention and also Luke, Ken, and anyone who could pass it on to any other aircraft or ground vehicle.

We were on our way. The great lumbering trucks in the rear, then Kevin, his stores, and shotgun in the next Rover, Beavis and Charlie with their heap of rations, stores, and moustaches next, then Alan and George with, in addition to supplies and radio, Alan's special sponge rubber elbow protection. I was bush-bashing in front with my instruments for star observations, stores, and a weeping wound. We all wore hobnailed blucher boots except Kevin who stuck to his strong engineer's shoes also used to sneak about quietly when he was duck shooting. The weather was growing hotter and hotter as the year wore on so that there were not many fleecy-lined leather jerkins in evidence. Kevin wore a rugged zippered jacket for shotgun cartridges and his R.A.A.F. peaked cap, while Beavis wore a wide-brimmed hat for the sun. Charlie couldn't possibly get a sunburnt lower lip it being always in the shade and George maintained his bare head and khaki drills, leaving Alan in a brand new Australian army slouch hat with the side turned up to let out the flies, khaki, and sponge rubber, and me in my usual uniform of rags, but still with a good belt-watch and penknife pouch. I never knew when I would have to improvise a leather wheel bearing.

The going was wonderful for Land Rovers for the first four and a half miles, being hard and level, but the heavy trucks, unable to negotiate the sharp turns we made to clear trees, simply had to mow them down. But then a relatively small sand rise cropped up across our path. We went over easily but the trucks stopped dead just as I had expected they would. After trying to extricate them for half an hour we let the tyres down and backed the trucks off the sand. Then Alan came to me with his hands on his hips, thumbs forward as usual, and assuming the look he'd seen on a sad bloodhound and practised for such occasions said, "What are we going to do?" "Point their radiators for the Kittens turnoff, give them a slap on the tailboards, and let them go"—I couldn't get it out fast enough. So we took what we could from among the heaped up scrub they had collected in the back and did just that. Much to the drivers' immense relief, I suspect. Fortunately Alan had previously arranged that O.C. Mallala would, in the event of an emergency, be ready to drop stores and fuel to us by Bristol Freighter.

We were immediately on our way south again feeling as if we all had a great weight lifted from our shoulders which, after all, was just about right. After twenty miles of reasonable going, the ridges began to assume tremendous proportions. This could only mean the close proximity of either a salt lake or claypan. Dusk was closing in already so we decided to beat our way through the high maze and camp on it if it were a claypan, beside it if it were a salt lake. As we slid down the steep sandy embankment, I jumped out to check it with a geological hammer before the others arrived. To my delight it was an iron-hard claypan, smaller than at Emu but still quite large, and as George had seen it from the air it was marked on his sketch. Throwing several dry branches across the bonnet for firewood, I drove fearlessly out on to it, went to its opposite side, turned, and pointed my headlights back to the party. One by one they came over the hill and stopped on the edge of the claypan.

Then Alan and I began our often used morse code messages with flashing torches or headlights switched off and on. He asked me if it were hard to which I replied "okay" and on they came to my still burning lights. We got the fire started as they circled around; out came the swags and food, and George set about preparing a meal. I didn't need an astrofix that night, so helped the people with flat tyres. Kevin took on himself the task of treating all the vehicles as if he had bought them himself and lay under each one checking drain plugs, leaks in radiator hoses, fan belts, oil lines, and the various levels of water, petrol, and oil throughout. Beavis rushed about helping everybody with everything, and Alan made radio communication to the waiting base station. It was a thoroughly great team and I knew everyone would be as eager at the finish as they were now. You could somehow tell.

During the radio contact it was decided to have Pete fly out in the little aircraft to try out the system while we were still only twenty odd miles away; he could bring some tins of petrol for us at the same time. We had only used about four gallons each but the standard rule is never to pass up a chance for more.

After all arrangements had been made by radio we ate George's frying pan full of good-tasting mysteries and drank a mug of tea each. The tea looked a little dark but we put that down to the inadequate lighting from a small bulb hooked to a battery, and the camp fire. On trying it I found it really was a little strong for me so I used it to wash my tin plate. Everybody readily joined in the clearing up and made the food safe from wild dogs or ants; bread and jam were wonderful for pudding, and we didn't want to lose a scrap. We had found by long experience that nothing on a motor vehicle was ever touched by ants even though the vehicle might be resting on an ant bed.

Next morning at first light George had a fire going and we were soon up plodding about, except Beavis who was springing about. Now it was daylight we wanted to check the claypan's length for a possible landing. Discovering it was more than ample we ran a centre line for Pete to follow by driving to and fro on the red surface many times with the Rovers. A few small golf-ball size stones had to be thrown clear, but otherwise it was perfect. By this time George had some wondrous porridge ready and also a panful of eggs—they wouldn't carry far in this heat and rough country anyway. I poured some tea he had made into my mug and it still seemed a bit strong so, after a tentative sip, I washed my tin plate with it again.

Shortly after we had cleaned the things and packed up the Rovers, we heard the purr of Pete's plane as it flew along the tops of the trees following our four Rover wheeltracks. This was now the time to heap our bundle of green mulga branches on the cooking fire to show Pete which way the wind was blowing. He came in to land. Once down he taxied back to us and switched off. He hadn't been too thrilled to be carrying a load of loose petrol in tins as he said it was like carrying a bomb ready to go off should anything happen, but he was immediately relieved of that and told he could bring supplies of water or food in future.

He said he'd been able to follow our vehicle tracks with ease, so all in all the operation had been a complete success. Then George asked him if he could go for a flip in the machine, and Pete agreed to swing the prop over for him. I jumped at the chance for an aerial look at the country ahead. It wasn't often I had such an opportunity so I climbed into the passenger's seat, rags, hobnails, and all, and Pete swung the propeller. Soon George and I were taxiing into position on the Rover centre-line; there he ran up the engine and let go the brakes. After the slow crawling through the bush for so long, this speed for take-off seemed almost supersonic, and I wondered if I had after all been a little too hasty. Good old George had us in the air safely, though, and we were flying off in the planned new direction of the ground party. It looked a bit rugged but that was to be expected, and some more claypans came into view after we had only been going ten or fifteen minutes.

Not wishing to use up too much of Pete's petrol, George and I agreed that we had got some practical help from the "flip" so he banked and started back on a reverse bearing. Soon we came to the camp claypan with the tiny Rovers dotted about, and George throttled back, lost height, and pulled down the air brake flaps lever over his left shoulder. When the trees at the over-run extension of our wheeltrack centre line skimmed beneath I felt myself gripping the seat more tightly than ever. In a second we were down, with the claypan racing past at a terrifying speed. I need not have worried. George slowed the engine right back and eased the plane to a stop, well short of any trouble. He taxied to the group waiting, locked on the brakes, released the flaps lever, and switched off. Still, my "Thanks, George," as I climbed out of my seat came in a voice three notes too high.

With that over we decided to be on our separate ways. Pete got in and was soon heading for Emu. We, too, got moving.

It took us several hours to progress as far as the little plane had taken us in fifteen minutes. At last we spotted the small chain of claypans through the bush; as we got to the top of a sandhill we saw them laid out before us. I stopped for the others and we all had a view of the "scenery," then made a fire to boil a billy for tea as it was past midday. We could feel that the days were definitely warming up now as we sat about eating some of Ozzie's fresh cooked meat, and bread and jam. George made the tea. This time I had nothing to wash up with it, so, resolving to observe him making it next meal, I poured it over the battery to wash off surplus acid. It looked like Indian ink as it spread over the brightly coloured cell caps. He might have invented something after all.

Just about everyone had colour cameras and I had a black and white one, so photographs for the recording of our trip were constantly being taken. None of us knew that we were on the brink of one of the most startling discoveries ever made on any of our expeditions past, present, or future, a discovery that would provide ample scope for all our cameras. George even had a colour movie camera—an instrument worthy of such a fantastic and accidental find.

We admired the visible terrain and slowly packed up again what little we had taken out of the vehicles for dinner. The remaining meat had already been securely tied up in several old flour bags to keep it safe from the persistent blowflies. Laboriously climbing into our Rovers, we started off down the sand bank towards the first of the small claypans.

15

Our Discovery of the Mysterious Aboriginal "Stonehenge"

From the foothills the first small claypan looked as though it might be salty, but after checking we found it was really as hard as the others, so we drove out over it. These stretches, short though they were, were always a relief from the hummocks of sand and fallen scrub. On this one it would have been impossible to land anything but a helicopter, as it was strewn with sizeable rocks and sharp stones, some joined to the solid underground strata, and it was very small, anyway.

It was back to the rough again as we climbed the bank on the western side, and trundled on. I often thought if a top gear wheel were to be examined on a recce survey vehicle, it would appear as new alongside a crawler gear from the same box. Within half a mile, a second, larger salt and clay mixture surface hard enough for anything to drive over crossed our path and we eased down the stony breakaway bordering the eastern rim. It was remarkably free from obstructions and almost capable of taking a light aeroplane landing, so to check its length by speedo tenths, Charlie and Beavis drove up and down its longest axis, while out of sheer exuberance, Alan and George raced their vehicles around it, in top gear for the second time in half a mile of travelling. I didn't move off course, being unwilling to alter my running speedo readings which I was entering in a book, alongside the compass bearing of present travel and a note about the topographical feature the reading represented. Referring to this at the end of the day enabled me to construct my own plotted path including the features, and when an astrofix was taken I could adjust the traverse from the previous star-fixed camp.

I did, however, have a brief scan of the rocky steep bank on the western side to find the best lead-out from this claypan. The small plateau beyond was roughly six feet higher than the level of the claypan. Dotted about with casuarinas or sheoaks it looked a very pleasant little spot. The shales seemed to have broken away to form an inclined plane which could be used as a ramp slightly to the south of where I was, so I started up and veered towards it to be in position at its base when the others were ready to follow. When they noticed my movement they made towards me so I started up the rough shale-strewn ascent.

The moment my vehicle topped the rise to level out again I saw it, spread out right across my path extending for at least sixty yards either side. It was almost like a picket fence with posts six feet apart made from slivers of shale. Tingling with excitement I switched off and leapt out of the cabin. Being in so isolated an area it was obviously an ancient Aboriginal ceremonial ground built by those primitive, stone-age nomads in some distant dreamtime. And here we were, surely the first white men ever to be gazing in awe at the sight, scarcely daring to breathe in order to hold the atmosphere of it all and to prolong the memory of this dramatic moment to its limit. The others had driven up the rocky incline and had stopped wondering for a fleeting instant what was the trouble, until they all saw the reason for themselves. We all knew without saying that it was going to cause much speculation and theory, and that we would all be recapturing this scene for years to come. Moved by curiosity, we ventured forward slowly on foot, as if we were creeping about an antique eggshell china shop.

Going right or left as personal feelings guided, the little party of Australians bent on finding something entirely different, and much larger, could not comprehend what they had stumbled upon. There was something eerie about this small pleasant plateau; the sun was not far past the zenith so the oaks were throwing full vertical shade. It was impossible to tell how old the posts were, but they must have been pretty old for they were well weathered at their base where countless ground thermals and wind currents off the claypan had sand-blasted them.

The area was about a hundred and twenty yards long, the main line bearing a few degrees west of north. The individual slivers of grey, water-impervious shale were protruding three feet above the surface of the plateau, and judging by the one or two which were leaning or fallen they seemed to be embedded about a foot or so beneath. Each was comparable in section to its neighbour, measuring four inches by three inches, very rectangular, and with a perfectly straight long axis. There were about sixty of them about two yards apart. As well as these there were clusters vaguely resembling stooks of hay each made up of one centre "post" of shale with a dozen or so slivers leaning in towards it, the inner ones resting against and seemingly propping up the centre; they covered a circle three feet in diameter and were three feet high. On closer inspection they seemed to be rather carefully placed. I counted half a dozen of these clusters in all, one placed at either end of the main line, at its centre, and one several yards distant on its own; the other two were on the plateau level on the eastern and western side. One of these was erected about fifteen yards west of the southern extremity but on a raised natural rock dais eight feet higher than the others, and what we took to be the main one of all was the cluster built roughly a chain west of the northern extremity.

Of course these discoveries were made over half an hour of careful exploring, which included the discovery of the obvious source of the shales used. There was still much of it lying about and jutting out of the sides of a small waterway which had eroded with the quick run-off from the few and far between downpours of rain. With each discovery the excitement mounted.

What were the characteristics and habits of these near mythical but very real builders? It would be fair enough to assume they were the same as those we see today in the bush. Were they familiar with the tribe that had left the yam stick near our recently made Coronation Parade? Possibly they knew them but only as a separate tribe; they were probably separated by some unseen boundary known to both over which neither must trespass for fear of certain death. This location would certainly have been absolutely taboo to any other tribe and probably also any women folk or children. It would in effect have been sacred, hallowed ground to be used sparingly and very reverently at important ceremonies. Their fires would have glowed in the night, maybe for weeks, while age-old rituals were in progress.

Fires! We must search for them—even the smallest evidence of buried charcoal—as modern scientists could deduce a lot from products of vegetable decomposition including charcoal. It was possible to tell how much time had elapsed since it had been a living branch. Some charcoal was finally found under the surface. With this carefully wrapped in rags and carried in a billy, we reluctantly turned our thoughts to our cameras. It seemed a horrible desecration to photograph the place at all, but we knew we must take shots from every angle, to give anthropologists and experts down in the impersonal cities material for armchair study. The word "city" suddenly seemed to put a bad taste in my mouth; it was incredible to think that this could be reached in an hour by jet plane from the heart of Adelaide, and yet it had not been seen until an hour ago.

At last the photographs had all been taken, and we sighed at the thought that there were still half a thousand miles to go and realized that we must be once more on our way. There was an ironic clash of old and new here, as only a few short miles away the first mighty atomic bomb ever to be brought to the mainland of Australia was to be blasted into immediate oblivion in several weeks' time, and it was by-products of this very weapon which could be used for determining the age of the charcoal from these prehistoric fires. I wondered what the scene would have looked like at night in those early days, with the ghostly sounds of the whispered chanting increasing in volume at times tapering slowly away, then surging back to life with the dancing of the black, naked participants, ochre painted and glistening with sweat in the glow of the fire. At the same time I couldn't help asking myself what these people, had they still been here, would have imagined if they had witnessed the glow from our atomic upheaval followed by earth tremors and shock waves.

We wended our way carefully through this Aboriginal "Stonehenge"—that was the name we'd automatically given it—and drew away from it into the west each with his own thoughts. I re-visited it alone five years later and carried out an astronomical observation to fix its geographical position exactly for all time. I also did a scale survey of it all and plotted it on the site using the tail board of my Rover as a desk. This was at the request of Alan Butement in Melbourne who had received repeated inquiries concerning it after it became known from our stories.

There was something like sixty miles to go to get to a pair of large salt lakes observed and charted by George on his air traverse. The northernmost one was named Lake Dey Dey, while the one about six miles to the south was called Lake Maurice. Nobody could say "Maurice" like Kevin. He was an expert and would use his brown hand to emphasize that the "ice" must be pronounced "ece." I had been formerly saying "Morris."

We had progressed about twenty-five miles that afternoon. The going was rough but parallel to the sand ridges. That is, it should have been parallel to the sand ridges but my vehicle compass indicated an upward trend with the result that we crossed over a few ridges obliquely. George said he remembered the ridges slowly dipping south of west to hit Lake Maurice without a single crossing. It didn't really matter, except that if we made a mistake it would take some time to correct it. Anyway, it was something to think about and discuss.

After tea I had just washed up as usual with my mug of Indian ink when Alan asked if I was equipped with a morse key on my transmitter. He was finding conditions poor for communications that night, and when I replied that I did have one he asked if I could ascertain if the base operator knew the code as some only worked on R.T. (radio telephone). Setting up the aerial I began transmitting on the key using C.W. (carrier wave). Finally we received a reply in morse—and the operator on duty was fully conversant with C.W. Unfortunately I was not as practised as the skilled operator who was punching out his message at machine-gun rate, so I called out to Alan, "Help!" He grinned as he came over and read it easily; he was as good as a trained operator himself, having had his own "ham" station once as a hobby. He was much quicker than I, and it was pretty to listen to.

It struck me that with this party combined, we could handle almost anything between us—apart from the question of the tea. I had seen George put two handfuls of leaves into a billy, an amount that would make a twelve-gallon oil drum of tea too strong. It was even too strong to wash up in—the end of my spoon was becoming dull—and once after the first mug had been poured, someone upset the billy, but no tea trickled out. It was too thick. We found that the hot leaves gouged out of the billy a handful at a time were wonderful for cleaning the greasy frying pan.

It was at this camp that I devised my bright idea. I would spirit away all the tea leaves in the camp into my Rover and at meal times when George asked if anyone had noticed the packet, I would "accidentally" discover a packet, bring it over, and throw into the boiling water my usual eleven separate leaves. Then I would place the billy right in a narrow strip of shade cast by a mulga branch, also by "accident," to make the coloured water appear darker. This worked perfectly for several days during which everyone suddenly took to drinking tea, even George who couldn't drink it before, as it "tasted queer." I spoilt it one day when I put in ten leaves because one had blown out of my hand, and what was worse I couldn't find any shade to place it under. Alan remarked that it seemed a bit weak then, so I took Kevin, Charlie, and Beavis into my confidence and we split up the job between us. It was getting to seem more than a coincidence that it was always I who noticed a packet of tea leaves behind a tree. When it all came out in the open with all its sordid details, George's laugh was the loudest, and to this day reminds me of my "shady tea."

Completing the full distance west by my compass we struck a huge salt lake at least ten miles long by half that wide, so with everyone happy again we turned on our next direction south. But, alas, another six miles brought us to the shores of an even larger one extending to a visible horizon in a glaring white shimmer of radiated heat. This was Maurice and we had in fact struck Dey Dey first after all. The extra tins of rations I had stuffed about the vehicle had attracted the compass and eased us over the several crossings to the northernmost lake. George had certainly got his own back over the tea episode.

This salt lake Maurice was as smooth as glass with minute blisters of pure dried salt covering the eighty or so square miles of it, and as we tentatively tried to walk on the surface they crunched like cornflakes. About six yards out the surface showed a tendency to break through so we hastened back to the Sahara-like bare sand dunes bordering the eastern side. There were rolling bare wind curved and smoothed dunes without a blade of growth on them for miles as far as the eye could see—a desolate-looking region if ever there was one. It was a good job it was only ninety-eight degrees for if it had been really hot it would have been unbearable.

Alan and George were busy with the radio ordering in a waiting Bristol from Woomera with cardboard storepedoes laden with tins of petrol, water, and food. The heavier ones were equipped with two store-dropping parachutes instead of the single one on the ration tubes. It had been arranged that the plane's side door be removed before take-off at Woomera as it could not, of course, be opened in flight for the drop. The eastern side of Lake Maurice was ample description of our location and we would let off a smoke generator when we saw them to pinpoint us. These lakes appeared on the standard world aeronautical series of maps of that area, rough as they were to date. We pushed southwards slowly and laboriously because of the dunes and hummocks alongside the lake. Alan finally tooted me to stop and came along proposing to try driving several yards to the west along the smooth edge of the pan instead of so tantalizingly close over the painfully rough ground. He had been on the radio during the time the rest of us had tentatively tried to walk on the cornflakes so was not aware of the treachery of the thing.

I flatly advised against it although I saw his so near and yet so far reasoning. He said that he would perhaps just try it for a second to see, and I repeated that I would not go near it for the life of me, but once he had an idea it was there until he *proved* it wrong. I could see him wavering at my insistence but he thought after all that he just might see for himself. I asked him at least to stay against the edge so we wouldn't have to cut too much wood to drag in to extricate his vehicle, not if, but when he became bogged. He climbed aboard, and Beavis, Kevin, Charlie, and I watched helplessly as he edged down. George was a Briton and jumped in with Alan. He went along at speed beautifully for the several yards it took him to pass us standing there, hearts in mouths, thinking how far we would have to be dragging the wood across the bare dunes in a second or so's time. As he raced past, he shouted out, "Look you blokes, no hands." The estimated second later as the tyres sank into the broken surface and the vehicle slowly subsided, I said involuntarily to the gathering, "Look you blokes, no Rover."

Alan would never ever try that again, we knew. Experience gained the hard way is always more effective. We rushed our vehicles in line obliquely a little forward and to one side of the stationary vehicle, stationary horizontally that is, and hooked each other up train fashion with tow ropes, tied one to the Lake Maurice model, and tried to help but it was like trying to pull a Cat 12 Road Grader over sideways with a pram. Unhooking, we rushed off over the dunes to look for wood, and all returned with huge bundles over the bonnets. George and Alan began shovelling in the jelly blue mud like fury. Beavis worked like a beaver, building a criss-cross corduroy wooden "road" in front of each wheel, while Kevin sank on his knees in the wet mud with a jack. I also shovelled a great hole to take the chopped length of wood, endeavouring to build a platform on which to place it. Charlie unloaded all the wood collected and raced off for more, wonder-

In our goon suits
Whatever happened to the bomb tower?

ing aloud why "the 'kangawoos' don't get stuck." Beavis grabbed his shovel and worked alongside Alan and George who were bullocking with logs and another shovel, at the other side.

With the passing of each minute the surface was moistening with the brine; we had stirred it up by clomping about on it. Kevin finally adjusted the jack and began levering only to push the wooden platform deeper into the mud. More wood was heaped on that as he got another length out of the jack and after five operations the "platform" and Rover went in opposite directions at the same rate. Several more tries had the Rover moving up as the mud, being close to the edge, gave up the battle. Good old Alan; he knew how to get bogged in the nicest way.

As soon as the weight of the vehicle was on the jack entirely, Beavis shovelled a tremendous hole around and well under, leaving the wheel in mid-mud. Long cross logs of Charlie's were placed transversely under it and on both sides, another layer at right angles over it, and so on, until no more would fit. The Rover was then slowly lowered by the mud-covered Kevin and to our delight the structure took the weight. We had already deflated the tyres to a few pounds and they spread out over the logs like wet dough. Good traction. Several hours later and an equal number of extra layers of mud over all of us, each wheel had been the receiver of a similar therapy, and now we were ready to hook up our train once more, and each slowly took the strain. Then at an accurate signal from George each driver, including Alan, let in his clutch and we gave it all we had at once. The Rover literally sprang out of the salt lake and bounced back up on to the smooth sand dunes which we had also levelled with our shovels, and it was out at last. It was twenty yards before I gave them the signal to stop. We switched off and danced about for joy in our heavy mud-caked hobnailed boots.

When the jubilation had died down Alan said two words full of meaning to the gathering—"thanks chaps"—then, as an after thought to me, "I think it would be a good idea if we avoided lakes like this in future." I agreed perhaps it would be at that, as we unhooked and "washed" the salty, muddy shovels and jacks in the dry sand and packed up. We couldn't resist a stroll back to the scene to look briefly at the excavation before we drove well away from the lake where none of us had left a fraction of our good humour, and were soon once again on our way.

The day had worn on for some reason and it was approaching camping time, but I was determined to get the most out of what daylight we had left. As I approached the mid-eastern half of Lake Maurice with the others coming along behind, I unexpectedly topped a higher sand dune and surveying the scene before me I burst into uncontrollable laughter, for spread out in front was a long claypan. Could we ever induce Alan to drive on it? Perhaps, at the point of Kevin's shotgun. I cascaded down the bank and a short check with a geological hammer proved it to be as hard as iron and capable of taking the weight of that fifty-ton Centurion tank at good old Area A, so I loaded on wood and drove out on to it as the others passed over the summit of sand. I'll bet they were laughing, too, but what a wonderful spot for our parachute supply drop the next day. I began nonchalantly lighting a fire as two of the vehicles came on. One seemed to hesitate on the brink—I think it was Alan's. He got out just to make sure—a wise move—and came over to join us, laughing as loudly as anyone.

We all had an excellent hot tea which we were more than ready for, and morale was at a peak as we yarned around the camp fire for a while before I thought it was about time I did an astrofix. Tomorrow we would be in the land of plenty again with full petrol tanks, and water tins, and different rations including some fresh from Woomera. I took out the theodolite to be ready for observing the stars. It just wasn't our day, what with Dey Dey first, then Maurice, and now as I looked skywards, wonder of wonders, clouds were appearing. By the time I was ready the sky was covered all over with snowy white rainless clouds, but no stars. It might clear enough soon, however, so I didn't pack up, and returned to the fire. Suddenly a large planet appeared in a small break for several minutes directly overhead. It was noticed first by Alan, who said, "I say! Lennie, what about *that* one?" then as it disappeared again immediately he added, "Sorry, old man." As I was explaining I wasn't so old as I still had my own teeth, the clouds cleared away as quickly as they had come and I got to work. After the sums and plotting during which everyone became motionless on their swags, I also gratefully sank down and was asleep before you could say "Alan Butement."

In due course we heard the drone of the faithful old Bristol Freighter as it approached and in no time it had found us on the claypan and was circling low overhead. Being the larger one we could converse direct with it by radio and save a smoke generator. They told us they would gain height so that the 'chutes would have time to open, and flew off rising all the time, until they turned, and, still rising slightly, made a bee-line for the claypan's centre. We were all at our Rovers, waiting to rush to each drop to check there were no split drums. Just at the right time out of the gaping hole in the fuselage, somebody pushed out the first cardboard storepedo and it arced towards the claypan. In a second a single parachute opened indicating a ration drop and the whole thing wafted gently down to hit the ground, crumple the cushion nose piece, and fall over under the fabric. Over we went, and quickly released the catches to unpack it on to the fabric to ascertain if everything was all okay. It was, so we told the radio operator, and added that we were ready for the next. This time it was two 'chutes, but one four-gallon drum of petrol still split. Righting it over a basin to catch the overflow we scratched a sign on the clay, indicating seventy per cent success. (We had somehow lost contact by radio.) After two more drops the operation was over and we were again in possession of plenty of water, food, and fuel—enough to reach the Nullarbor Plain and Transcontinental Line where there was a series of sidings roughly forty or fifty miles apart. The trains Controller had already been advised to give us all possible assistance when contacted by Don Burnard's telephone line.

As soon as we farewelled the Bristol with grateful thanks, we discarded rotten green, mouldy, or iron-hard bread for fresh bread, refuelled and emptied the cans of water into our containers, bundled the still usable 'chutes into our vehicles, and pushed on again without more ado. There was a nightmarish belt of saw-tooth mountains of sand between us and the Nullarbor according to both George's map, and George who had seen it from the air, and we were anxious to come to grips with it and get it over. Apparently they were only fourteen miles across in a straight line, but this fourteen-mile stretch was to be really something.

The "mountains" started about twenty-five miles to the south so I was anxious to cover that distance before nightfall and camp on the northern start of them to be ready to attack them fresh and early in the morning with cool engines. From the air it had appeared first-class going over gravelly plains, which observation proved to be quite correct.

The twenty-five miles from the Bristol aeroplane's supply drop, fell behind us quickly. The red, still-shimmering mass ahead grew in detail as we approached with the sun dipping. It was a definite line capable of accurate plotting on maps of almost any scale, so we stopped dead still in daylight for a change. I scanned from side to side carefully to select a likely lead-in to them, and seeing a slight diminishing in height of the first in one place veered towards it and camped at the foothills. Alan and George pegged down a large white canvas outline of a square with strips brought for such purposes, to mark our lead-in point at the camp, so H.Q. could be informed accurately in the event of an unforeseen happening of any kind in the belt requiring air support. The rest of us set about the tasks with the vehicles—refuelling, slackening all tyres to twelve pounds pressure, filling radiators, checking oil levels very carefully, and getting some fresh food on to heat for tea. When finished they radioed news of our position to base and gave details of the square which could be easily picked out from the air. Afterwards we lay down very early so that we could have a good long rest before the earliest possible start in the morning.

16

The New Permanent Site

Before first light we already had the fire going, breakfast finished, and everything packed up. As the terrain became clearly visible ahead we moved off around the canvas square and began the first ascent.

We topped the first sand ridge reasonably easily and I touched the button on the sheep dial tally counter taped to the steering column to read One. These sheep hand counters come in useful for many things other than sheep, such as counting the number of radio beats on some types of time signals used in astrofixes, and counting the number of sandhill crossings in a given distance— fourteen miles in this case—for future reference in the event of a recrossing or access road work assessments. At the top of each rise, without slowing or losing momentum, I always flicked my eyes along the next ridge and veered towards any saddle or diminishing of height in order to better our chances of crossing it. The sandhills were only fifty yards apart so this had to be done in the several seconds before the Rover began its descent and my view was obscured by the large strong sun visor which I had designed and made under the watchful supervision of Sam Milbourn, the foreman of our valuable motor workshops in Adelaide. Some of the ridges here started before the previous one ended, while some had a hundred yards of flat valley separating them but it was virtually one after the other all the way. They were free from spinifex hummocks and much more devoid of growth than most of the others further north. That made them easier to negotiate because there was that much less to interrupt momentum—the only factor which carries one over.

As soon as we reached the saw-toothed summits we slid down the other side amid a fall of loose sand. With my one set of wheeltracks over, the next vehicle could follow more easily, and so on, until Kevin who carried the heaviest load. Progress was exceptionally slow—often we had to make as many as fifteen attempts, gaining a few inches each time. Eventually, we reached a point of no return. We could no longer see the plain behind us and in front the same desolate scene of red sandhills stretched to meet the sky line a mile away.

The heat in the oven-like cabins was almost unbearable as the screaming engines became burning hot. The sand ridge belt viewed to the east or west from any summit, had the clearly defined profile of the teeth of a cross-cut saw, which could be seen for many miles either way rearing up into the blue sky. These were without a shadow of a doubt the worst sandhills I had ever seen and I have not seen any quite so stark and high since. They fused together, some jumbled so thickly there were dunes upon ridges, and at the centre they reached ridiculous proportions. No ordinary wheeled motor vehicle could have negotiated them, but all our Rovers fought back faithfully. On a visit to the factory in England later, I was well qualified to hand out bouquets without reservation to their chiefs.

The sheep counter was running hot, reading over a hundred already, and although the speedo said ten miles we had penetrated only about a third of the way. The sand ridges are caused by the wind from the Nullarbor Plain; the sand spilling down the far side of each ridge as it is blown across shows the direction of the prevailing currents, consistent for centuries at right angles to the long axis of the ridges. They present a real challenge to man and machine and I knew at least where an access road from the Transcontinental Line to any possible new testing site would *not* be made.

With our persistent battering the speedo eventually read fifteen miles which I guessed to be the centre of the fourteen-mile belt, so we stopped for a dinner camp. We mended several flat tyres under the scant shade of a quondong bush while George, who by now had the packets of tea back in the tucker box, got the billy on. Alan tried the radio and reported that we seemed to be able to see some sand from where we were. Beavis got some labelled sample bags of soil, Charlie gave the opinion that even he, unorthodox as he was, couldn't land an aircraft here, and Kevin's "hobs" protruded from under each Rover in turn.

After lunch, which consisted of some cold meat, a lump of bread and jam, and a mug of shady tea, the radiators had cooled sufficiently to enable the caps to be removed and the radiators topped up with water. Half-way through a second lump of bread and jam, George said "Come on, let's get it over with," so with the food stuck in my mouth, I started up and charged the next ridge twenty yards in front slightly obliquely with a sort of ramping pattern reserved for the larger ones.

Search, veer, sheep counter, slide, charge, repeat, search, veer, sheep counter . . . so it went on into the afternoon; shoulders and arms ached from fighting the wheel against loose sand, and the accelerator pedals were as shiny as mirrors. Then suddenly from the top of a dune—no, it couldn't be, but there it was again— we caught a fleeting glimpse of the Nullarbor Plain above the further line of ridges, with its straight-edged horizon meeting the dome of the brassy blue sky. Then it was gone as we half slid and half drove down the side amid a fall of sand. On the next dune we had a longer look at the Plain, then more and more became visible as each summit was won until we were all aware that the end was in sight. The speedo read twenty-five miles from the canvas square and it was four o'clock. We'd have to try to make the Plain before nightfall as none of us wanted to camp in these "mountains," to wake up in the morning with another at our Rover doorstep, if we could possibly help it. Also, I had determined to force myself to carry out another astrofix that night and for this I wanted to be on the flat, so that I could calculate an exact bearing across to the nearest siding on the railway line. After all this weaving about I couldn't really say where we would come out, and as our petrol was literally pouring through the carburettors, we couldn't afford to do too much meandering about the Plain looking for a siding. The railway was located over thirty miles from the finish of the sandhills anyway. Anywhere straight south would bring us to the line, but then which way would it be, east or west to the nearest siding? I knew it was going to take every effort I could muster to keep awake long enough, for we'd travelled a hundred and fifty miles from Emu, and I had been bone weary even before we left, but there was just nothing else I could do.

That was tonight and this was only four in the afternoon with five miles of dunes yet to handle. I glanced behind again, not to make sure the others were following but to see the sandhills that we had crossed. They seemed to rear up like a disappointed ogre, realizing that they had been beaten for the first time since they'd got together. I knew for a fact that we would never try to beat them again.

As we neared the plain, which until now had looked like a shimmering grey devil's billiard table, we were able to discern small hardy bushes a foot high. It was all over bar the last few dunes. The speedo showed that it was going to be at least thirty miles of travel from the canvas square fourteen miles back, and the sheep counter would read about two hundred and fifty to three hundred crossings. As suddenly as they had begun, and just as dusk was quieting our numbed brains and tortured bodies, the sandhills came to an end, and in ten yards a distant flat skyline of level rock with occasional undulations stretched out before us. It was amazing, this precise line of demarcation between sandhill and level ground. Nobody wanted to move another inch as the realization that the nightmare was behind us was followed by such a sudden relaxation in built-up tension and anxiety.

I asked Alan if he would save the radio sked until the morning

189

Blast the Bush

as he could by then include our exact latitude and longitude to base. The vehicles were still almost glowing hot and so there was nothing Kevin could do in the way of repairing them. Charlie had no aeroplane handy, Beavis couldn't dig a sample hole if he tried as we had forgotten to include a jack hammer, and apart from George's tea leaves and my theodolite all the chores were willingly shelved for the morning.

I guessed that we would be heading for the sidings at Cook or Fisher but which one and in what direction I couldn't say. Every bone in my body ached, as did, I suspected, every bone in the camp, but I set up the instrument, rolled out my swag to sit on while I made the calculations, received the time signals, and got on with the fix.

Eventually, finishing the observations to the bare minimum number of stars possible, I left the instrument set up while I sank down to work. Everyone was sound asleep; how I envied them. When I had successfully worked out one latitude star I used that value obtained to solve the longitude ones, and arrive at a solution. But the position emerging was an impossible one. It showed we were camping in some town hall near Kalgoorlie. I must have been more addle-headed than I had imagined, so I worked out a second one. This showed from a plot on the aeronautical map that we all were in church at Port Augusta. I bowed my head, but not for long in case I fell asleep. Then I checked another latitude star. Thank heavens it agreed exactly with the first. I staggered over to the instrument to read another longitude star and then staggered back to work it out again. Good grief! We were now in the middle of the Indian Ocean.

Nothing like this had ever happened in my life before so I concluded I must be very very dazed. Indeed I felt a lethargy creeping over me and the pencil dropped from my nerveless fingers. So I pushed everything off my "bed," weighted the lot down with rocks in case a sand-dune-forming wind should spring up, and fell back in my rags and boots on to the canvas. As I fell

190

I noticed a torchlight flashing from Alan's swag; he was sending morse of all things so as not to waken the camp. I doubted if even McWilliams with a plug of gelly could have done that. "What is our fix?" it spelled out. "I haven't the faintest idea," I signalled back as I completed the fall to the canvas and shut my eyes.

Within a minute I was sitting up again, book across my knees, retrieved pencil at the ready, and working like a slave. Of course! There is an astronomical triangle to solve in this, known as the P.C.Z. (in that order) triangle for longitude observations, but at Tallaringa I had been doing similar observations for bearings which are solved by reversing the triangle to Z.C.P. This is the one my fuzzed mind had hit on first, and it had become clear as a bell the second my head hit the pillow. I rose quickly before dropping off and worked out the whole three stars to agree with each other beyond any doubt. A lot depended on this position, so I plotted it there and then and scaled off a careful bearing (for checking in the morning). Fisher turned out to be at a distance of thirty-two miles. I even dragged myself to the instrument which I had left for a sun observation and carefully placed it in its box with loving care. With everything else safe I again lay down, this time completely contented; it was midnight by this time and that was the last I knew.

As the sun peeped up above the Nullarbor horizon, I had the feeling someone was close by. It was Alan Butement mooching about my swag, hands on hips with thumbs to front, waiting for news as soon as my eyelids flickered. I set his mind at rest straight away with my "secret of success at last" story and he was transformed in a second to an overjoyed herald as he hurried off to inform the camp that it was still "rather fun finding out where you are."

The whole atmosphere was no longer "gloom" and I found it impossible to remain on the ground although everyone had had five hours sleep up on me. Soon the pigeon-hole jobs had all been

taken care of and we headed off in a bee-line for Fisher. Ten miles
went by in forty-five minutes. Then we noticed the formation of a
dust blizzard coming at us from the west. It grew blacker as it neared
and we stopped to see that everything was secure with all vents
and windows shut tightly. It hit with the fury of a tornado,
rocking the Rovers on what was left of the springs as we crawled
slowly forward into it in a sort of eerie semi-night, with the sun
a blood red disc. I concentrated on my compass as each Rover
almost bumped into the next in line—we were afraid of losing
each other on the plain in the swirling dirt and sand.

In an hour it had gone, and in that time we had only travelled
two miles. According to my calculations we had twenty miles
to go and in another hour and a half we saw the few shimmering
fettlers' huts dead ahead, thanks to that good old P.C.Z. triangle.

It was a weary, ragged, and red-eyed group who chugged into
this "civilization" with the name Fisher (to my relief) on a railway
sign. There were four huts—two were to live in and two somewhat smaller ones were outhouses. How such flimsy-looking
structures ever survived the dust storm we didn't know. A
grizzled old fettler who greeted us said that he had heard along
the line that we were due, and advised us that a train was coming
from the west that evening if we wanted it stopped for any reason.
Alan and George decided to go on it as more could be gained by
the organization of air support at Woomera by George, and Alan
as Chief Scientist had been away from Melbourne for some time
now, and his office must be stacked with papers demanding his
attention.

During our recce up to now we had come to the conclusion
partly from our air surveys, and partly from our studies on the
ground, that an area north of Ooldea on the railway line looked
the most promising. Kevin, Charlie, Beavis, and I would therefore
carry on in one Land Rover each to examine this area. We were
all sorry to see them go; we had come over two hundred miles
from Emu together—it had been the kind of ordeal that makes

life-long friends. George got out his best shirt and Alan clutched his billy of charcoal from "Stonehenge," and after sorting out some gear and making a few verbal arrangements we awaited the train's arrival. George put on his last billy of shady tea for this trip for us, and we had a meal in the frying pan on the fettlers' stove indoors. Much as we liked barbecues this was a novelty.

From Fisher the full circle of flat plain was broken only by the railway line which disappeared to a pin-point either way, and this meant that the light from an approaching train could be seen for an hour before it finally drew up. The train controller had been contacted at Port Augusta and our request had been passed on to the diesel electric train driver to stop at Fisher. They didn't often have visitors there, strangely enough. There was a drum of petrol for their section rail car from which we would refuel, vouching to return a full drum from Woomera. The headlight of the train began to glimmer but with the last night's work after the sandhills I couldn't keep my eyes open any more, so with farewells and handshakes and thanks all round I crawled to where my swag was unrolled in a corner of the hut, and fell asleep among the mice there. Just before I succumbed, I heard George apologizing to Kevin for whipping off with his share of tinned pineapple.

The following morning the four of us drove in an easterly direction alongside the line. Eventually we arrived at the next siding of Watson which had six houses—too much civilization to take in all at once. When we pulled up a smiling German migrant family came forward to greet us. The father could speak a little English, but the others spoke to each other in German only. As we stood in a group a little girl clutching her mother's apron said something in rapid German to which the mother replied. I remarked to our group what a clever little girl she was to be able to speak German so well at her age. Kevin hasn't stopped laughing about that to this day.

Soon we drove on the twenty-two miles to get to the next

siding of Ooldea where we had planned to launch our attack into the bush to the north. Little did we all dream that that sleepy little siding of Watson was to be *the* one ultimately selected for the siding to serve the future permanent British atomic bomb testing site. This site was to be known as Maralinga, after a native word meaning "thunder." We couldn't imagine at this stage that we would be surveying a bitumen road from here to the new site, that a theatre would spring up, and that there would be a huge fuel depot, dozens of store sheds, an immense stone crusher, an earth moving plant, and hundreds of men. It still seems fantastic to me as I remember our little ragged group of four as forerunner to such an enormous project.

As we pulled into Ooldea we noticed that it must have been the first or last siding on the actual Nullarbor Plain depending on which way you were travelling, as the "beach" dipped sharply to cross the line a hundred yards east, with oaks, scrub, and sandhills beyond. We were getting used to those huge "towns" by now. (This one had two rows of houses.) At the appearance of the ganger we stopped and once again grouped around. When he had asked us a few questions I thought that I would have some fun with him and told him that ninety trucks were following us and were all converging on Ooldea. We laughed as he raced away yelling, "Hey! Flossie, what do you think . . ."

As we camped there that night all the neighbours dropped in to listen to our travel talks, each bringing some cookies, and Les and Flossie made the shady tea while we lay on their veranda. It was a big night in all of our lives and more welcome than any stiff and formal dinner party where people don't seem to be appreciated in rags and hobnailed boots. Heaven knows what they'd do if they had to make an emergency leather wheel bearing seal. We had already satisfied all their curiosities concerning the ninety trucks, not realizing ourselves how close to the truth we would have been had we repeated that in a year and a half's time.

Plunging directly into the bush to the north again first thing in the morning we found ourselves into the sandhills almost immediately, and in a few miles saw the last of civilization in the form of the desolate-looking Ooldea Aboriginal Mission. Composed of several cottages and a small fenced-off soak in the middle, the completely deserted settlement was ringed by high, quite bare and loose sandhills, which had crept with the winds to leave only half the normal height of the houses protruding from the Sahara-like dunes. The sand was already level with the windows and the tops of the front doors.

Pressing onwards to some likely markings on George's aerial drawn map, we easily negotiated one sandhill crossing after another. There was a profusion of growth here binding the sand together and the hills were diminished in height; we only needed four attempts to surmount each one. Suddenly after twenty miles an almost unheard of miracle occurred. Black clouds appeared and it began to rain. It pelted down in bucketfuls making the sandhills as hard as concrete. It was easy to drive over them, but the valleys became one long series of bogs. We pulled each other out with the rain washing our "clothes" as we hooked up the tow ropes at each bog, and Kevin, Charlie, and Beavis were as exuberant and full of fun as ever. They were men you'd choose to be shipwrecked on a desert island with, as the saying goes. The bush took on an appearance of gloom as the thick black scrub vanished in a mist of rain in all directions. I was, of course, relying completely on my compass for direction. More than one experienced bushman has become "slewed" and travelled in a circle in a featureless maze of wet scrub, with a full black sky. With all the towing we had only progressed twenty miles when it became darker. It was after five already, so we stopped on a raised flat out of the path of the main waves. I began thinking once more of the prehistoric man's beach.

I carried a little canvas tent especially for nights like this one but so far I had never used it. Now was a good time to start and as I put it up, the others rigged canvas camp sheets from Rover to trees and from vehicle to vehicle. We suddenly heard a laughing shout from Kevin who took the bread that we had collected from the Bristol and tied to the roof of his Rover in a box. Opening it up he saw a soggy fused mess which would have been ideal for the fowls but jam would only sink through it like hot butter. You couldn't help laughing as Kevin held handfuls of it up and what didn't ooze through his fingers, washed off with the rain. It was a forlorn looking but jolly quartet who huddled in my tent to eat a tin of cold stew each and drink a mug of water which had just come from the sky. After a tired talk about how we were supposed to find an atom bomb site the world would all know about, they all went "home" early and soon the camp was silent, its exhausted but still good-humoured occupants asleep.

The rain abated some time in the night. We packed up in a sunny cloudless morning after a rather moist breakfast of once dry biscuits and jam followed by water from the mugs left out overnight. Then we hit the invisible trail. In four hours the scrub stopped dead and the ground was covered in open saltbush undulations. We all knew immediately that this was going to be the place. It was wonderful to see it rolling away to the north as it did, and we carried on into it on that historic day in October 1953. After several miles we saw scrub ahead and to the east so we veered to the west, and the saltbush undulations rolled away as far as we could see, even through our binoculars from the top of a flattened gentle rise. It opened out to the left and right as well; apparently we had stumbled into it at its most south-easterly point. I stopped when we arrived at a long, flat tableland rise and they all drew up alongside. We solemnly wrung each other's hands and just gazed about us in all directions for half an hour. The depressions were accompanied by two foot high bluebush and saltbush with some clumps of mulga, and although I hadn't as yet visited Devon, I could imagine that it was something like this! The herbage was of a different nature but the open undulations were there just the same with the hedge-like growth in the dips.

We erected my transmitter aerial there and then on this raised tableland and soon had George at the microphone at the base station at Woomera. We told him the news, saying that we would contact him soon. He replied that he would have a railway line "grader" devised in the workshops to smooth out a possible landing field as Charlie advised him this was quite possible with the mile-long potential runway we were talking from at the moment. George would drop it from an open door'd Bristol in a free fall as soon as it was made; by then we would have a centre line pegged out with white rag markers to follow. We would take turns dragging the grader back and forth with our Rovers one width at a time, by the mile-long speedo distance. Beavis was the active one here studying the "excellent soil," when scraped smooth, for the plane's support, and we all agreed that we would have an aircraft landing in several days after George's grader fell out of the sky. Driving down a hundred yards or so to a smooth firewood-laden depression we spread our still wet things about to dry and made a roaring fire. This area proved to be six hundred feet above the level of the Nullarbor Plain and after the rain we were beginning to feel the cold.

It was an elated though beaten up group of four who had a hot meal, mugs of shady tea, and a long yarn around the fire as they waited for dry blankets to flop into on that eventful night. Today was to determine the actions of thousands of men, and to be responsible for the spending of many millions of pounds in the time to follow, but we nevertheless lay down—Charlie in a "kangawoo's" pit that he had found—and slept the sleep of reward for our efforts.

George had apparently worked at Woomera throughout the night with some welders and workshop men to have the grader made and ready; he also made sure there were forty-four gallon drums of petrol and water and stacks of extras needed for an official visit to the area by Sir William as soon as we gave the word. All but the grader were padded for shock; some bundles were attached to anything up to three 'chutes, and he reported to us over the radio next day he was all ready to have the flight leave on the following morning. We found the site on the table-land a hundred yards away from our camp easily the best and had a good centre line marked picking the best axis and several measured indicators either side to give us the right overall width. We even had time to make a slight exploration of the area to the west as there was supposed to be a well dug by an explorer, Tietkens, in the 1890s, shown on old compilation maps as Tietkens's Well. He had accompanied Ernest Giles on some hard trips of discovery in Central Australia and his operations brought him from the natives' soak at Ooldea to here. I still have an impression in relief on wood grown over a tree blaze that he had done in 1889. It was simply his initial "T," and 5.89 (May 1889).

Sure enough we found his wells, one forty feet deep and the other a hundred feet deep, timbered and with remains of his old camp alongside. These would be our prized relics to show the visitors during the "tourist" season in several days' time. All this was reward enough for what we had gone through.

Mid-morning found us waving to the Bristol which had arrived to our radioed astrofix of the night before and soon a message came over the radio to us to mind our eyes as the railway line grader was to be pushed out on its water pipe rollers on the next low run over. Old George thought of everything. I had been wondering how they were even going to move such a weight out of the plane when the exact time came. It was going to be heavy enough for the four of us on the ground.

The radio asked how it went as it had hit the ground and reared up end over end to come to rest with a clang and we replied okay as they gained height for a forty-four gallon drum drop. Out it came on the next high run. Unfortunately the two 'chutes opened one at a time so that terrific strain was thrown on the first and it was torn off; the second was also torn off leaving the drum ringed in old motor tyres padding to come as a free fall. It hit with an ear-splitting noise and the once round drum finished up dead flat with no ends. They tried again; this time the 'chutes tangled, streamered, failed to open, and we were now in possession of two flat drums instead of one. Saying that they would try a load of goods the next pass, they dumped a great black bundle which spun end over end rolling the 'chutes up, and it hit the saltbush with a resounding crack and half buried itself. When the plane's radio operator inquired hesitantly how it went, Charlie had had enough and told them, "Quite poor—we haven't got anything so far."

One tin of fuel and one of water that came next were successful, and the plane headed for Woomera after a lowest of low passes. We all squirmed and ducked, all except Charlie who had often done the same thing himself chasing his "kangawoos." On inspection of the black bundle that had been dropped we couldn't identify anything until someone noticed some charcoal. It was a wood cooking stove rolled up in a huge tent between two folding tables and some stools, and there were some rations in a potato bag. So much we gleaned from twenty minutes detective work, but what a messy wreck! We photographed it and went to assemble the grader.

In two days of non-stop work with Beavis in his element, we had the strip completed. We took our turns at dragging the grader back and forth, sometimes with two Rovers at a time when the debris heaped up too much. A Bristol came from Woomera with George and party to test it out for a landing. The test, with my school friend Len Murphy flying, went off without a hitch. Unloading *gently* an assortment of gear similar to the first lot, they departed for Emu to fetch Sir William, John Tomblin, and others to inspect our area. Next morning after we had built a small camp with everything we had to hand the plane returned with the party and came in for a perfect landing once more.

There followed a reasonable tour of inspection in the next few days, a quick trip back to the gravel plain south of Lake Maurice, and forty miles west with John Tomblin "just to make sure," but there was of course no comparison between these areas and the one we were camped on. Kevin's and my Rover reared up at the sight of the start of those sandhills and refused to go another inch, so we returned to Tietkens's Well area. I assured them I could make an access road to it from Watson or Ooldea and Sir William summed it up with, "It's the cat's whiskers."

During our tour of the fringes and into the scrub we came upon a most pathetic sight. On the ground side by side were two very old but definite mounds of dirt one six feet and one three feet long. On the longer mound lay an ancient weathered spear alongside an old split woomera or spear launcher, while on the smaller lay a spear half the length used as a toy by the little native boy who must be lying beneath. Probably they were both struck down by thirst, disease, or spear wounds, and were buried alongside each other in separate graves, with their sole meagre possessions resting on the surface. We drove away slowly, careful not to disturb anything, and returned to our camp.

Maralinga had been born. Sir William long in need of an "atom" trim sat on the pile of rubbish from the air-drop as I cut his hair with my ever-present hand clippers. This was done under a battery of movie cameras.

Finally the time came to fly back to Emu where the atomic bomb was all ready to go. Our work finished here, I climbed aboard the aircraft on Sir William's "orders" to fly back with them to prevent any likelihood of my missing the detonation of the bomb, for which we had all worked so hard. My Rover followed on another trip by the Bristol which landed equipped with a loading ramp.

I little knew then that within the course of the next year, both Len Murphy and our unconventional pilot friend, Charlie Taplin would both be dead. Len was killed when a wing fell off a plane

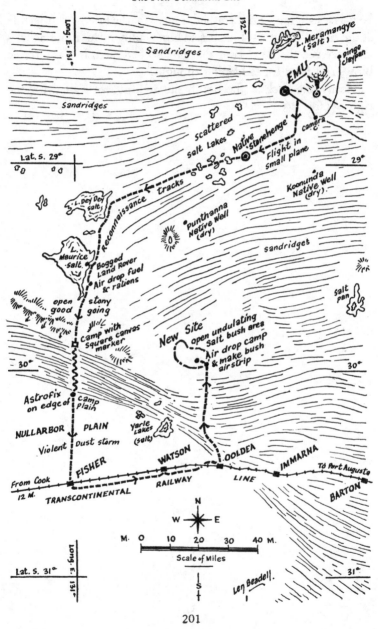

L. Meramangye
(salt)

dingo
claypan

EMU

Long. E. 131°

132°

Sandridges

Sandridges

scattered
salt Lakes

Native
'Stonehenge'

camera

Lat. s. 29°

Reconnaissance   tracks

Flight in
small plane

29°

L. Dey Dey
salt

Koonunda
Native Well
(dry)

Punthanna
Native Well
(dry)

L.
Maurice
salt.

Bogged
Land Rover
Air drop fuel
& rations

Sandridges

salt
pan

open
good

stony
going

Camp with
square canvas
marker

New Site

open undulating
salt bush area

Air drop camp
& make bush
airstrip

30°

30°

Astrofix
on edge of

camp
Plain

NULLARBOR   PLAIN

Violent   Dust storm

Yarle
Lakes
(salt)

From Cook

FISHER

WATSON

OOLDEA

IMMARNA

To Port Augusta

12 M.

TRANSCONTINENTAL   RAILWAY   LINE

BARTON

N

W   E

M. O   10   20   30   40 M.

Scale of Miles

S

Len Beadell.

201

he was test-flying, and it crashed. I saw Charlie briefly in Adelaide at the end of the year—I identified him readily by his moustache—and received the news later that he also had died. It was a tragic blow, and food for saddening thought.

Meanwhile back at the bomb site at Emu we waited for the right winds.

17

The Atomic Climax

There was an air of expectancy and excitement in the whole camp. Everything was in place and ready at every installation. The underground structure at the end of the co-axial cable which we had blown out was crammed with instruments and a movie camera. All the toothpaste tubes had been inserted in the baffle plates and the camera towers were equipped with their dozens of cameras, some colour movie, some fast, others slow—every combination possible. Each would be automatically set going at the time allotted to them before and during the final count-down.

Maddock's "stuff" was in place and had proved its efficiency in many exhaustive tests. Loudspeakers had been placed in mulga trees wherever they would be needed and wired to Maddock's microphone at the firing panel, while both ends of every forward building had been removed. Each vehicle scheduled to be up front on the day had been identified and labelled with a large white number or letter fashioned on the passenger's windscreen with sticking plaster and the respective owners and passengers listed. Every man in the camp was listed and was ordered to be in a special position at the count-down, to be checked off on duplicate lists by section heads and the security boys.

Already full-scale rehearsals had been carried out to the letter. Even to the time when everyone would be up by midnight and off in their fuelled vehicles to carry on with their respective tasks, loading each camera with live film, joining wires at the tower base, locking the massive steel doors of all the underground concrete block houses. Maddock and Frank Hill were in place at the firing desk and vehicles and personnel double-checked. In fact everything had been done except arming the bomb which was hoisted, harmless, to the top of the tower. This proved the winch arrangements. The engines in the Centurion tank were started up for tests to observe whether they would continue moving or be snuffed out, and it was even equipped with "Cecil," the straw dummy propped up at the controls. It has been stressed before that this tank could have been placed in a position where it would have melted, but more knowledge could be gained if there was something left of it to study. Each group listed to be in possession of the personnel keys was handed them; after the rehearsal they were checked off by Maddock who was powerless to do anything unless he had regained charge of each one. This also went for the master key held by the men on top of the tower.

Nothing must go wrong when the moment arrived. An enormous responsibility rested on every man because even a day's hold-up at this stage meant thousands of pounds. The main problem was the weather, for if the wind was not exactly from the right quarter nothing would induce anyone to consider the explosion. Actually the final decision rested with Sir William alone. After all, the eyes of the world were upon Emu Claypan at this stage. Newspapers from every country which continued to pour into the ante-room, had headlines such as, "Penney's packet ready to go"; one with three inch high black lettering read, "Tomblin—Wind still wrong," and so it went on with cartoons and facts which only helped to heighten the excitement to fever pitch at our "haunted goanna hole" village.

Slowly and dramatically the hours ticked away into days until one evening a weather prediction was handed in saying that the wind was going to come from the south-east the following morning. That was the news around tea time. The weather boys both at the site and everywhere in the Commonwealth were the ones governing this phase of the procedure—a job few would envy.

On this night, however, tomorrow seemed to be *the* day, and everyone in the camp was so tensed up that I doubt if one member had even the suggestion of sleep before midnight when the activity was due to begin. The decision was being backed by each weather report that came in. Seven o'clock was the time scheduled for the firing in the morning, but even that time would not stand if any doubts whatever arose. When these electronic timing wizards said seven o'clock they really meant it, with some fantastically small proportion of a fraction of a second for tolerance, and the equipment was checked and rechecked by an automatic system coupled up to a precision time signal. Nothing that could possibly be done electronically was done by hand—tense nerves gave too great a margin for error.

On the stroke of midnight as if everyone had not been studying a watch dial for hours, an ear-splitting siren sounded out over the camp and loudspeakers boomed; the final preparation had officially begun. Fully clothed men were in their vehicles which were abrim with petrol in minutes, and off they went to their well-rehearsed jobs. I took my old Rover and reported to the small group who had drawn our personnel key while the other keys were being given out to the correct people. The battery of rockets was connected to the system, cameras were being carefully loaded by trained fingers, the cipher room which somehow had an open line of communication to U.K. was buzzing with excitement; this was near the hydrogen loading meteorological balloon building, from which balloons were being sent up at a great rate to be tracked by met. theodolites and radar to their limit of height.

Cooks, mechanics, and men who could stay at the village to lessen the quantity of checking work at Area A were out but still had to be marked off the lists. In fact they were to obtain a more spectacular view of the fireball and mushroom than anybody. The double loudspeakers wired to the trees made the trees look as if they had enormous ears.

There was no rush or panic as each man methodically went about his role in this drama of dramas. I had said, when I was

asked, that I should like to stand on the bluff if it were feasible—
I knew it would give a good commanding view of the scene. It
appeared that that was where Sir William, Luke, and a selected
group would be standing as well, so my ideas conceived when
this was all virgin country were being maintained to the very end.
In fact everything that had been done through the year had
confirmed my mind's eye picture.

The darkness wore on with lights from vehicles and torches
flashing about in the mulga. At dawn, when grey streaks of light
heralded the commencement of this most historic day in Australia's history, my allotted group gathered to proceed to the very
base of the bomb tower. The ominous black shape had been
winched up to the top and was now a fixture. Three intrepid
scientists were readying it for the last time. As I saw the tremendous steel structure of the tower I recalled my guess as to the
ultimate damage it would suffer. Top blown off, middle third
strained, and lower third barely marked. I also remembered the
grinning faces which informed me "You'll see." I hadn't long
to wait.

We got out, leaving the engines running, and secured two
wires at the foot of one of the legs and joined them up securely.
In the micro-second of detonation this device would send a
container, which would snap shut in a calculated fraction of a
second, through the atomic cloud and high into the air, clear of
the heat, with the object of collecting radioactive dust and sealing
in a small portion for later studies. We jumped into the Rovers
waiting three paces away and as we sped off I took a last glance
back at the dreadful black mass at the top of the tower. What
was it capable of?

Back at the hut housing Maddock's stuff, a growing collection
of personnel keys appeared near the row of key holes, but still
the gaping hole where the master key fitted was empty. With
half an hour to go, I drove up to the bluff to get into position.
I aimed the rear of the vehicle to the tower as I wasn't sure what

would happen to the glass windscreen. Various clipped sentences came from the loudspeakers explaining each particular phase. At this stage I was issued with a pair of arc welding goggles. Sir William greeted me and we recalled how we had stood on this very spot discussing aspects of the project exactly a year before. How much had happened since!

Phase Wallaby or some such Australian animal name had now begun and the time seemed to be racing. Through binoculars I looked at the tower four and a half miles away, and could easily make out the bomb mass that gave it a top heavy appearance. Sir William told us to be careful in the use of the goggles. He did not think it was entirely a good idea to look at the fireball at the instant it formed, so everyone was to be facing exactly in the opposite direction to it. Only after the flash could they turn around with safety to observe the formation of the mushroom. I was told that to look at the flash would be like looking at the sun itself from a few miles away, and I began to wonder at the wisdom of being there at all. There were five minutes to go which meant the final count-down would begin in a minute.

At last the clipped "four minutes to go" came over the air for all to hear, including the Canberra jet bomber streaking across the sky, scheduled to rip through the atomic cloud, when it rose high enough. The pilot was to fly away from the bomb in the last few seconds before the explosion, then bank when he saw the flash, and guide the Canberra at full throttle through the centre of the mushroom, snap shut some wing-tip canisters, and report to a coupled tape recorder any sensations he felt as he flew through the mass. He was then to scream at wide open throttle to Woomera where a cordoned-off area at the end of the cleared strip would be his parking place, and tumble out to a waiting ambulance for immediate medical checking. The plane would be attacked by a scientific team equipped with goon suits and geiger counters and studied minutely from nose to rudder while the wing-tip containers were handled by other experts loaded with instruments. The value of the results of such a test were obvious. Flying into such a cloud of unknown composition called for sheer courage but many volunteers had come forward.

"Three minutes to go!"

There was no doubt about it—the atmosphere at this time was hushed; everyone had his own imagined idea of the outcome. There had been an intense build-up to it all, starting from the day of the Eyebrows conference with Bill Worth as far as I was concerned, and with the first invasions for everyone else. The seconds ticked away on the belt watch I was clutching; the welding goggles lay loosely around my neck. I wasn't going to risk the use of them at all after Sir William's remark.

"Two minutes to go!"

This was fast becoming unbearable. Maddock's stuff began actuating on its own the things designed for it. I could picture his control panel, keys turned on over the master key in place, rows of lights flashing from phase to phase, and Frank Hill anything but "gloomy" flicking his eyes over the dials and cathode ray patterns.

"One minute to go!"

I nearly jumped a foot as it penetrated that the end of eternity was so close; I had been too busy thinking to look at my watch. Suddenly an Admiral covered in braid standing alongside me turned to Sir William. "I say," he said "what if it doesn't go off?" Sir William gazed sleepily at him over the top of his black-rimmed glasses and broke the silence of the group with his confident and almost yawned reply, "It'll go off all right." That was that—emphatically. I couldn't have come out with a question like that, at a time like that to the man on whose shoulders the complete burden rested, for all the shady tea in China. Kevin Connolly had arrived, and as Sir William added, "This isn't my show, I'm just here for a look," Kevin whispered to me, "It takes a big man to say that."

"Thirty seconds to go!"

Someone pulled his collar up around his ears as you would to keep out a cold evening and it struck me it wouldn't help much unless it was made of reinforced concrete. Hardly anyone wears a reinforced concrete collar these days anyway.

"Twenty seconds to go!" Silence!

"Ten seconds to go—nine, eight, seven, six, five, four, three— a loud generator started up alongside me and I nearly died on the spot, as I flicked an eye on the tower and back again before he continued, two, one, NOW!!

Great Scott, what a sight! The entire sky as it domed out and down past the distant horizon lit up in a blinding flash of fire and we felt the heat on our backs for a fleeting fraction of a second. No noise yet, apart from the screaming jets of the Canberra bomber, as it made its run in. In just over a second we all whirled around to witness the end of the fireball and the boiling cauldron of deadly radioactive dust fighting for room to expand all at once. It surged, enlarged, and began its skyward path to write its mushroom signature in the heavens.

The bright sun was about twenty degrees high by now in an otherwise cloudless burnished sky and the mushroom began to obliterate it as the screaming silver streak of the Canberra closed the distance to the thickest part of the mushroom. We saw it again as it raced out of the other side and rose above the line of the mulga trees. As it banked the pilot indicated that he was going to have another go at it. Then, without as much as a goodbye, his silver bullet lit out for Woomera.

Gosh! what a morning. During all this we had temporarily forgotten that there was supposed to be a noise and shock wave accompanying it, but we were soon reminded. At least there was a little warning—we saw a difference in colour of the mulgas as they bent reflecting the sun at a different angle. This change in colour from normal dull green to almost light grey neared slowly at first as we were looking at it obliquely. Then when it got to within half a mile it seemed to race at us and we were nearly pushed over by its force. The blast was the loudest I had ever heard; it sounded like a case of gelignite let off by Chinny in a room.

It was over. The results of a year's all-out effort manually and mentally gone in the fraction of a second. But what a climax! It surely lived up to and surpassed our wildest guesses, and one and all agreed that they were proud to have been associated with it.

Old Luke had a little joke waiting at this stage for the reporters. "Look," he shouted pointing at the atomic cloud, "do you see it?" Everyone whipped around to direct their attention to the cloud. "A perfect portrait of a myall blackfeller written with

atomic dust; the new and the old have come together today."
He was so enthusiastically serious that one by one they agreed
that there was no doubt about it. Sure enough the newspapers
printed the huge headlines: "Myall black man written by atomic
dust in sky over Emu." Good old Luke.

Suddenly—for all this interchange had only taken several
minutes, Sir William leapt into a waiting vehicle and raced for
the cipher room. Churchill in U.K. probably had the news
minutes later on the wide open line from the haunted goanna
hole to him. I drove back to the Claypan where there was a York
plane waiting with engines going, and George Pither and
several others, including me, crawled aboard, and we waited
for Sir William before taking off for a quick flight over the
scene. It was still a very hot radioactive area and we lacked the
speed of the Canberra, but all the danger of the cloud had dis-
persed by now.

The York was lined up at the right end of the strip for the
light breeze. Then we roared off down the runway for an
immediate take-off. Flying to the forward area took a couple
of minutes, but soon we were looking down at the devastation.
Small fires were burning, and long radial streaks of bare destruction emerged from a centre. It looked as though a giant paper
bag of grey flour had been dropped and had burst.

Where was the tower? There was absolutely nothing whatever
left at the centre of this schemozzle. Just smooth saucer shaped
ground. I couldn't believe my eyes . . . that huge steel structure
which I thought might become a little "strained." . . . I laughed
aloud at my naïvety. The whole thing had melted and vaporized
in a decimal of a second; later, when I visited the scene in a goon
suit, it still seemed impossible.

I was sitting next to Sir William as he looked down over
his glasses. I saw him rubbing his hands and heard him murmur
one word, "Whacko!" He should have been an Australian.

We felt the plane bank as we came over for a last glimpse of our year's work. Then back to the Claypan where we and aircraft were run over with geiger counters. They did not respond.

Frank Hill came to me with head bowed, eyes lowered, and uttered a long, soft, drawn out "Gloom!" He had lost a prized lizard in the fuss. In a day or so Sir William boarded a special aeroplane and began his return journey to England to wind up the details on paper. He farewelled me in his tent saying that we would meet again in due course at Maralinga.

Later that morning I was talking to Maddock in his tent, and the sight of his diary gave me an idea. It lay open at the present day's date, 15 October 1953, and, while his back was turned, I helpfully entered up for him his movements of the day:

> "Up early to darn my socks, brush teeth, and fold my washing; let off atom bomb and iron my hankies."